LOVE & LEMONS

POP *of* FLAVOR

LOVE &

PO

FLA

JEANINE DONOFRIO
WITH PHOEBE MOORE

LEMONS

P *of*

VOR

100 Saucy, Spicy, Crunchy, Herby, Tangy Recipes for Craveable Everyday Cooking

PHOTOGRAPHY BY EVA KOLENKO

AVERY – an imprint of Penguin Random House – New York

AVERY
an imprint of Penguin Random House LLC
1745 Broadway, New York, NY 10019
penguinrandomhouse.com

Illustrations by Stephanie Worthington and Trina Bentley

Book and cover design: Make & Matter
Food stylist: Marian Cooper Cairns
Food styling assistant: Natalie Drobny and Paige Arnett
Prop stylist: Genesis Vallejo

Library of Congress Cataloging-in-Publication Data

Names: Donofrio, Jeanine author
Title: Love & lemons pop of flavor : 100 saucy, spicy, crunchy, herby, tangy recipes for craveable everyday cooking / Jeanine Donofrio.
Other titles: Love and lemons pop of flavor
Description: New York : Avery, an imprint of Penguin Random House, [2026] | Includes index.
Identifiers: LCCN 2025039969 | ISBN 9780593853146 hardcover | ISBN 9780593853153 epub
Subjects: LCSH: Vegetarian cooking | Vegan cooking | LCGFT: Cookbooks
Classification: LCC TX837 .D63225 2026 | DDC 641.5/636–dc23/eng/20260106
LC record available at https://lccn.loc.gov/2025039969

Printed in China
10 9 8 7 6 5 4 3 2 1

The authorized representative in the EU for product safety and compliance is Penguin Random House Ireland, Morrison Chambers, 32 Nassau Street, Dublin D02 YH68, Ireland, https://eu-contact.penguin.ie.

To the *Love & Lemons* readers

CONTENTS

CHAPTER 4:

HERBY

CHAPTER 5:

TANGY

CHAPTER 6:

SWEET

When I first fell in love with cooking, it was part of a bigger love story.

A story about my husband, Jack, and me, and a time in our lives when we were falling in love with each other, with wandering farmers markets, and with spending long nights in the kitchen together. We had always liked trying new foods, but at some point, the act of cooking itself became part of the fun.

I started cutting out of work early. I'd stop at the store for that night's cooking project and then head home to start prepping. Chopping onions and garlic became my meditation. Then Jack would walk in, and we'd open a bottle of wine, play music, make a mess, eat way too late, tag team the dishes, and take forever to clean it all up. The next night, we'd do the whole thing over again, exploring new flavors and recipes.

Fast-forward to now, and dinner looks different. It's rushed. It's loud. It's the opposite of leisurely . . . because—you guessed it—we have a family. Our evening meal is less of a creative ritual and more of a functional act that has to occur after snack time and before pajama time.

For our first few years as parents, this put me in a serious cooking rut. I found myself making the same go-to dishes night after night, relying on the same familiar flavors. I was eating just to eat. As someone who was used to finding so much joy in the kitchen, I felt completely blah about it.

I needed a new strategy—but not a complicated one.

It had to be a flavor-boosting, easy-to-pull-off approach that would keep our family dinners running smoothly while making cooking (and eating) fun again.

I started asking myself, "*What do I actually crave—and why?*"

I thought about my favorite take-out dishes. I'm always excited to eat the saucy pasta from the place down the street, or the noodles with the crunchy, spicy topping from our go-to Thai spot. If Jack suggests ordering Mediterranean, I say yes immediately. I can't wait to dig into a falafel wrap loaded with tangy pickles. **I realized something: often, one special component is what makes these meals irresistible.**

That realization shifted everything. What if I focused on flavor-packed components in my own cooking?

I started experimenting in the kitchen again, making punchy sauces and crunchy toppings that I could keep on hand for several days to jazz up a variety of meals.

For example, I drizzled Creamy Corn Sauce (page 44) over nachos one night and then mixed it into a comforting orzotto the next. I tossed Coconut Curry Peanuts (page 150) into a fresh cabbage salad and used up the rest on a weeknight noodle bowl. I began leaning on store-bought flavor boosters too, spooning chili crisp over my morning eggs and mixing harissa into soups and stews. I quickly realized that even the simplest dishes could be elevated with just a swoosh or a sprinkle.

I wrote this book to share this component-based approach with you. It got me out of my dinner rut because it gave me a new way to cook the kinds of meals I crave. I hope it helps you add a pop of flavor to your everyday cooking too.

COOK WHAT YOU CRAVE

HOW THIS BOOK IS ORGANIZED

A typical cookbook organization? No! This is a fun book!

Instead of organizing the recipes into chapters by meal type, I group them by texture and flavor so that you can cook what you crave:

SAUCY

SPICY

CRUNCHY

HERBY

TANGY

SWEET

Each main chapter highlights four or five components I love. I share three full recipes that feature each component, plus a handful of other tasty ways to use it to punch up simple meals.

For example:

Make the Red Pepper Tahini (page 24) from Saucy. Then . . .

- Try one or more of the three recipes that follow—the Saucy Skillet Chickpeas (page 27), the Ricotta Arugula Pizza (page 29), and/or the Cauliflower Pineapple Kabobs (page 31).
- Still loving that sauce? Check out page 32 to find five additional ways to use it!
- Of course, I hope you'll come up with your own creative uses too.

Then, flip to a different section, try a new component, and do it all over again!

Cook once, eat twice!

How many times have we all bought a jar of something for one recipe, only to never touch it again?

In the last few years, I've started paying closer attention to the condiments I keep on hand. I only buy ones that match my cravings (hello, chili crisp!), and I find ways to use them often.

The same goes for the homemade components in this book. If I'm making Smoky Potato Tacos (page 91), I'm not just prepping the Jalapeño Radish Pickles (page 88) for that night. I'll use them the next day on a noodle bowl, and a few days later, I'll toss them into a salad for a tangy, spicy kick. Cook once, eat twice! (Or three or four times . . .)

I've always been a little meh about meal prep, but prepping components is a flexible, flavor-forward strategy I can get behind. When you have an exciting topping, sauce, or spread on hand, creating delicious meals is simple.

I hope you embrace the cook once, eat twice mentality as you cook your way through this book. Don't let that last bit of Spicy Turmeric Paste (page 118) or Creamy Kimchi Sauce (page 275) waste away in the fridge. It's ready and waiting to liven up your next meal!

10 FLAVOR ESSENTIALS TO KEEP IN YOUR KITCHEN

Flipping through this book, you might notice that there are a handful of pantry ingredients I use over and over again. For example, tamari brings savory depth to the cold udon on page 93, the lettuce wraps on page 153, and the kimchi soup on page 279. Miso adds salty, umami oomph to the cherry tomato sauce on page 56 and the turmeric paste on page 118. And fresh lemon juice and zest brighten up, well . . . at least half the recipes here. (It's Love & Lemons, after all!)

These ingredients aren't the star components that I've built this book around. They're just pantry basics I always keep in my kitchen! *But without them, I couldn't cook flavorful meals.* They give me an amazing foundation for creating bold flavor.

Want to set yourself up for flavorful cooking too? Stock up on these 10 essentials:

1

Lemons and limes—You probably won't be surprised to learn that I always have lemons and limes in my fridge. :) I think a squeeze of lemon or lime juice is the simplest way to add a pop of bright flavor to any dish. Always buy whole fruits instead of bottled juice. The freshly squeezed juice tastes fresher and lighter, and you get the added bonus of the lemon and lime zest, which is packed with bright flavor as well.

2

Vinegars—When I want to give a dish a sharper, tangy kick, I turn to vinegars like rice vinegar, apple cider vinegar, and balsamic. I also keep distilled white vinegar on hand for making pickles, like the Pickled Sweet Corn on page 250.

3

Tamari—Tamari is a Japanese soy sauce with an intense savory, umami flavor. I often use it in Asian-inspired recipes or when I want to add a "meaty" taste to plant-based ingredients like mushrooms (see the pulled mushroom sandwiches on page 111).

4

White miso paste—This Japanese fermented soybean paste is another plant-based umami powerhouse. I love using miso in sauces and dressings, for its texture as well as its flavor. It thickens my Bursty Cherry Tomato Sauce (page 56) and makes the sauce on my Broccoli Miso Noodle Bowls (page 157) lightly creamy.

5

Tahini—This Middle Eastern ground sesame seed paste has a buttery mouthfeel and slightly bitter, lightly nutty taste. A fabulous base for dressings and sauces, it's hands down one of the most-used ingredients in my kitchen. I find that different brands vary quite a bit. My favorite is Seed + Mill, which has a delicious, rich flavor and smooth, creamy texture.

6

Full-fat coconut milk—Creamy, rich, and fragrant, full-fat coconut milk can transform into a flavorful broth, curry, or soup in minutes. Be sure to buy canned coconut milk, not the kind in a carton, which is generally less creamy and contains more additives.

7

Fresh ginger—Ginger's refreshing bite is one of my favorite flavors, and it elevates both sweet and savory recipes in this book. A knob of ginger will keep for about a week in the fridge, but pro tip: You can also store it in your freezer for months. No need to thaw before grating!

8

Spicy peppers—Sometimes a little heat can really bring a dish to life, so I always keep a jumble of jalapeños, serranos, and Fresno chiles in my fridge. Don't let these peppers scare you—I find that jalapeños are getting less and less spicy these days, so they're more approachable than they used to be. Also keep in mind that chiles hold most of their heat in their seeds and membranes. Feel free to remove these parts of the peppers to make them milder.

9

Whole and ground spices—A well-stocked spice drawer gives you so much freedom to play with different flavors! I typically use ground spices like cumin, turmeric, and cardamom, but in a few places in this book, I call for whole spices like fennel seeds and coriander seeds. Punchier than their ground counterparts, they're a great way to level up the flavor in your cooking.

10

Pickled red onions—If you've never made pickled onions, head to the kitchen and whip up a jar ASAP. Sweet, tangy, and, well . . . oniony, they give a restaurant-worthy burst of flavor to sandwiches, tacos, bowls, and more. And guess what? They're super easy to make! Here's how I do it:

PICKLED ONIONS

1 small red onion, thinly sliced
1 cup distilled white vinegar
1 cup water
2 tablespoons cane sugar
1 tablespoon sea salt

Place the onions in a lidded 16-ounce or similar-size jar.

Heat the vinegar, water, sugar, and salt in a medium saucepan over medium heat. Stir until the sugar and salt dissolve, about 1 minute. Pour over the onions.

Set aside to cool to room temperature, then cover and chill in the refrigerator for at least 1 hour or overnight before using. Store in the refrigerator for up to 2 weeks.

Seasonal cooking is flavorful.

A lot has changed since I wrote my first book, *The Love & Lemons Cookbook,* ten (!) years ago. I moved from Austin to Chicago . . . and back again, I became a parent, and more.

But through all that change, one thing has stayed the same: I love cooking with seasonal produce.

It all comes back to flavor. Vibrant heirloom tomatoes from a Michigan farmers market in August *taste better* than ones from the grocery store in winter. Stubs of corn wrapped in plastic will never measure up to the sweet, juicy ears my mom picks up from the farm stand down the road from her house in late July. Fall butternut squash has bright orange, creamy flesh; spring asparagus is crisp and grassy . . . you get the picture.

To be clear, I know that eating local, seasonal produce isn't always possible. (Spend a winter in Chicago, and you'll figure that out pretty quick.) Nearly all the recipes in this book will taste great with regular grocery store produce.

But I hope you'll still shop for the local, seasonal stuff when you can. Like any of the components in this book, it's a simple way to make your meals more flavorful and fresh.

Now, let's cook!

CHAPTER 1

RED PEPPER TAHINI
EGGPLANT YOGURT SAUCE
CREAMY CORN SAUCE
BURSTY CHERRY TOMATO SAUCE
GUIDE TO GREEN SAUCES

Saucy

A delicious sauce is the #1 way to make any meal more exciting (and easier, if you prep the sauce ahead). You'll find some of my favorites in this chapter. Get ready to dip, swoosh, douse, and drizzle!

RED PEPPER TAHINI

I've created countless sauce recipes over the years—this red pepper tahini might be the boldest, brightest yet! Loosely inspired by muhammara, a Middle Eastern red pepper dip, it stars roasted red peppers (for sweet and savory flavor), tahini (for richness), and pomegranate molasses (for a delicious sour pop). For a sauce that tastes so complex, it's incredibly simple to make. Blend up a batch in 5 minutes or less!

TIP

You can find pomegranate molasses in some well-stocked grocery stores, Middle Eastern markets, or online. Its distinct sweet-and-sour flavor really makes this recipe pop, so it's worth seeking out. But in a pinch, you can skip it; double the honey and add an extra 1½ teaspoons fresh lemon juice to the sauce.

- 1½ cups jarred roasted red peppers
- 2 tablespoons tahini
- 1 tablespoon extra-virgin olive oil
- 1 tablespoon fresh lemon juice
- 1 tablespoon pomegranate molasses
- 1½ teaspoons honey
- ½ garlic clove
- Freshly ground black pepper

In a blender, place the red peppers, tahini, olive oil, lemon juice, pomegranate molasses, honey, garlic, and several grinds of pepper. Blend until smooth and season to taste.

Store in an airtight container in the refrigerator for up to 5 days.

YIELD: ABOUT **1¾** *CUPS*

VEGAN: Use maple syrup instead of honey.

GLUTEN-FREE

STAUB

SAUCY SKILLET CHICKPEAS

WITH RED PEPPER TAHINI

This saucy chickpea skillet is everything I want on a weeknight—it's fast, it's filling, and it's insanely flavorful. I briefly simmer canned chickpeas in my red pepper tahini sauce, then pile on fresh toppings to create a delicious, scoopable meal (crusty bread for serving is highly recommended). This recipe is simple enough that you could blend up the sauce and cook the chickpeas all in one go, but for super-quick assembly, make the sauce ahead.

1 recipe Red Pepper Tahini (page 24)

⅔ cup water

3 cups cooked chickpeas, drained and rinsed (page 320)

¼ teaspoon sea salt

3 red radishes, thinly sliced

½ cup crumbled feta cheese

Chopped fresh parsley, for garnish

Fresh mint leaves, for garnish

Extra-virgin olive oil, for drizzling

Lemon wedges, for squeezing and serving

Aleppo pepper

Crusty bread, for serving

In a medium skillet, combine the red pepper tahini and water. Add the chickpeas and salt and stir to combine. Bring to a simmer over medium heat and cook, stirring occasionally and reducing the heat as needed, for 10 to 13 minutes, or until the sauce is thick and creamy. Remove from the heat and season to taste.

Top with the radishes and feta and garnish with parsley and mint. Drizzle with olive oil and squeeze lemon juice on top. Sprinkle with Aleppo pepper.

Serve with crusty bread and lemon wedges.

SERVES **4**

VEGAN: Skip the feta or use vegan feta. Use vegan Red Pepper Tahini (page 24).

GLUTEN-FREE: Serve with gluten-free bread.

RICOTTA ARUGULA PIZZA

WITH RED PEPPER TAHINI

On the weekends, I often have my sister and her family over for homemade pizza nights. I always make a simple cheese pizza for the picky kids and an exciting, veggie-driven pizza for us adults. This pizza has become one of our favorites. It starts like a basic white pizza, topped with creamy ricotta and nutty provolone, but after it comes out of the oven, I punch it up with a drizzle of red pepper tahini and a shower of greens. A little sauce goes a long way here, so if you have extra, flip the page and make those delicious veggie kabobs. Cook once, eat twice!

Cornmeal, for stretching the dough

1 pound pizza dough, store-bought or homemade (page 323)

¾ cup whole milk ricotta cheese

Heaping ½ teaspoon lemon zest

½ teaspoon sea salt

1 cup grated provolone cheese

1 Fresno chile, stemmed and thinly sliced

¼ cup Red Pepper Tahini (page 24)

1 cup arugula

Extra-virgin olive oil, for drizzling

Lemon wedge, for squeezing

Fresh basil leaves, for garnish

Preheat the oven to 500°F.

Dust a baking sheet with cornmeal. Place the pizza dough on the baking sheet and stretch it into a large oval. Use a fork to poke holes all over the dough. Bake for 7 minutes. Remove from the oven and leave the oven on.

In a medium bowl, stir together the ricotta, lemon zest, and salt. Spread evenly over the par-baked pizza crust, leaving a ¾-inch border around the edges. Top with the provolone and sliced chiles. Bake for 8 to 10 minutes, or until the provolone is melted and the crust is browned and cooked through.

Remove from the oven and drizzle with the red pepper tahini. Top with the arugula, drizzle with olive oil, and squeeze lemon juice on top. Garnish with basil, slice, and serve.

SERVES **2** *OR* **3**

TIP

High-protein tofu has a firm and chewy texture straight out of the package (no pressing required!). It holds up well on the grill, and it crisps up nicely when baked. I call for it in a few recipes in this book. If you can't find it, use pressed extra-firm tofu instead.

CAULIFLOWER PINEAPPLE KABOBS

WITH RED PEPPER TAHINI

Consider red pepper tahini your summer sauce. It goes well on any and every vegetable you'd want to grill—zucchini, mushrooms, peppers . . . you name it! I especially love it on this sweet and savory combination of cauliflower, red onion, tofu, and pineapple—the sweetness of the pineapple really pops against the rich, tangy sauce. Just add a side of rice or farro for a refreshing summer meal!

¼ cup extra-virgin olive oil

½ teaspoon garlic powder

½ teaspoon onion powder

½ teaspoon za'atar (optional)

1 small cauliflower, cut into florets

10 ounces high-protein tofu, patted dry and cut into 1-inch cubes

8 ounces fresh pineapple, cut into 1-inch cubes

½ medium red onion, cut into 1-inch pieces

Sea salt and freshly ground black pepper

Cooking spray, for the grill

Red Pepper Tahini (page 24), for drizzling

Fresh cilantro leaves, for garnish

In a small bowl, mix together the olive oil, garlic powder, onion powder, and za'atar, if using.

Thread the cauliflower, tofu, pineapple, and red onion onto metal skewers. Brush with the olive oil mixture and season with salt and pepper.

Preheat a grill or grill pan to high heat and spray with cooking spray. Grill the skewers for 3 to 4 minutes on the first side, or until char marks form and the tofu releases from the grill. Rotate and grill for 2 to 4 minutes on each of the remaining three sides, cooking until well charred.

Transfer to a serving platter and drizzle with red pepper tahini. Garnish with cilantro and serve with more red pepper tahini on the side.

SERVES **4**

VEGAN: Use vegan Red Pepper Tahini (page 24).

GLUTEN-FREE

MORE WAYS TO USE

RED PEPPER TAHINI

+

On a DIY grain bowl.

Choose your favorite grain + a veggie + a protein . . . Just add this sauce for a flavor-packed meal!

+

On a gooey grilled cheese sandwich

with fresh mozzarella, thinly sliced red onion, and a handful of spinach.

+

Over any roasted vegetable.

I especially love roasted carrots and cauliflower with this sauce. Top with toasted almonds or Spiced Almond Crunch (page 160) for a next-level side dish!

On a vibrant summer salad.

Toss grilled summer squash and zucchini with white beans, toasted pine nuts, and the lemon vinaigrette on page 282. Drizzle with red pepper tahini and garnish with soft, leafy herbs.

On a veggie sheet pan dinner

made with roasted chickpeas, broccoli, and big crumbles of feta.

EGGPLANT YOGURT SAUCE

Whenever I have the oven on in the summer, I'll roast an eggplant alongside whatever I'm cooking so I can keep fresh baba ganoush on hand. I often add yogurt for creaminess and tahini to make it a little richer. Depending on what I'm using it for, I'll sometimes thin it into a drizzleable sauce—which is how this eggplant yogurt sauce came to be. The eggplant and a touch of smoked paprika give it a delicious smoky flavor. To make it even smokier (or to avoid turning on your oven in the summer), cook your eggplant on the grill. The timing will vary by grill—just cook until it's well charred, soft, and collapsed.

- 1 large eggplant (1½ pounds)
- ¼ cup whole milk Greek yogurt
- 2 tablespoons extra-virgin olive oil
- 2 tablespoons fresh lemon juice
- 2 tablespoons tahini
- 1 garlic clove
- ½ teaspoon sea salt
- ¼ teaspoon smoked paprika

YIELD: ABOUT **1¾** *CUPS*

VEGAN: Replace the Greek yogurt with silken tofu.

GLUTEN-FREE

Preheat the oven to 475°F and line a baking sheet with foil.

Pierce the eggplant several times with a knife and place on the baking sheet. Roast for 20 to 30 minutes, or until completely tender and collapsed. Remove from the oven and set aside to cool.

When the eggplant is cool enough to handle, peel off and discard the skin. Measure 1½ cups of the soft eggplant flesh and transfer to a blender. Add the yogurt, olive oil, lemon juice, tahini, garlic, salt, and smoked paprika and blend until smooth. Season to taste.

Store in an airtight container in the refrigerator for up to 4 days.

GRILLED ZUCCHINI GYROS

WITH EGGPLANT YOGURT SAUCE

I have a thing for messy sandwiches. Maybe I'm making up for being an unadventurous plain turkey sandwich eater as a kid, but now I like my sandwiches with extra sauce and extra napkins. Case in point: these wraps. Zucchini planks are marinated with gyro-inspired seasonings, then charred until tender and wrapped up with fresh herbs, bright pickled onions, and a good douse of eggplant yogurt sauce. If I'm grilling for a group, I set out all the components and let everyone assemble their own gyro. This also works great for advance meal prep—store the grilled veggies and sauce in separate containers and assemble when you're ready to eat.

2 tablespoons extra-virgin olive oil

2 tablespoons fresh lemon juice

½ teaspoon dried oregano

½ teaspoon garlic powder

½ teaspoon sea salt

¼ teaspoon dried thyme

¼ teaspoon ground cumin

Freshly ground black pepper

3 medium zucchini and/or yellow squash (about 1 pound), sliced lengthwise into ¼-inch-thick planks

4 pitas, lavash, naan, or other flatbreads

¾ cup Eggplant Yogurt Sauce (page 34)

½ cup sliced jarred roasted red peppers

½ cup Pickled Onions (page 19)

Chopped fresh dill

Fresh mint leaves

Aleppo pepper

In a small bowl, whisk together the olive oil, lemon juice, oregano, garlic powder, salt, thyme, cumin, and several grinds of pepper.

Place the zucchini in a large shallow dish and pour the marinade on top. Use your hands to coat, then set aside to marinate for 15 minutes.

Preheat a grill or grill pan to medium heat. Working in batches if necessary, grill the zucchini for 2 to 3 minutes per side, or until char marks form and the zucchini is tender but still has some bite. Grill the flatbreads for 1 to 2 minutes per side, or until warm and soft.

Assemble wraps in the flatbreads with a slather of the eggplant yogurt sauce, the grilled zucchini, red peppers, pickled onions, dill, mint, and pinches of Aleppo pepper. Serve with any remaining eggplant yogurt sauce on the side.

SERVES **4**

VEGAN: Use vegan Eggplant Yogurt Sauce (page 34).

GLUTEN-FREE: Use gluten-free flatbreads.

FALAFEL-SPICED SHEET PAN FRIES

WITH EGGPLANT YOGURT SAUCE

We love falafel, we love fries . . . and we REALLY love a sheet pan meal, so here's a fun, easy way to enjoy all three together. Spiced potato wedges are drizzled with creamy eggplant yogurt sauce and topped with everything you'd pile on falafel—think cucumbers, tomatoes, pickled onions, and lots of fresh herbs. Serve it as an appetizer or dig in for dinner. If you want to add a little protein, sprinkle crispy chickpeas on top.

4 medium russet potatoes (2¾ pounds), cut into wedges

2 tablespoons extra-virgin olive oil

1 teaspoon garlic powder

1 teaspoon onion powder

1 teaspoon sea salt, plus more to taste

Freshly ground black pepper

½ teaspoon ground coriander

½ teaspoon ground cumin

½ cup Eggplant Yogurt Sauce (page 34)

2 tablespoons water, plus more as needed

2 Persian cucumbers, diced (about 1 cup)

½ cup diced cherry tomatoes

½ cup Pickled Onions (page 19)

¼ cup chopped fresh parsley

Aleppo pepper

½ cup fresh mint leaves

Preheat the oven to 450°F and line two baking sheets with parchment paper.

In a large bowl, toss the potatoes with the olive oil, garlic powder, onion powder, salt, and several grinds of pepper. Spread evenly on the baking sheets and roast for 25 minutes, then flip the potatoes and rotate the pans in the oven. Roast for another 15 to 20 minutes, or until crisp and well browned on the outside and tender in the middle.

Remove from the oven and let cool slightly. Combine all the potatoes on a single baking sheet and toss with the coriander, cumin, and a pinch of salt. Spread evenly on the baking sheet.

Place the eggplant yogurt sauce in a medium bowl. Stir in the water, adding more as needed to reach a creamy, drizzleable consistency.

Drizzle the sauce over the fries, then top with the cucumbers, cherry tomatoes, pickled onions, and parsley. Sprinkle with Aleppo pepper and top with the mint. Season to taste and serve.

SERVES **4**

VEGAN: Use vegan Eggplant Yogurt Sauce (page 34).

GLUTEN-FREE

CRISPY PITA SALAD

WITH EGGPLANT YOGURT SAUCE

It's an understatement to say that my co-author, Phoebe, and I love salads. Between prior books and the blog, we've written more than two hundred salad recipes! This one is a riff on fattoush, a Levantine salad made with fried pita. When we first combined our creamy eggplant sauce with the crunchy spiced pita, crisp veggies, tangy feta, and sweet dates, Phoebe took one bite and exclaimed, "This is my new favorite salad!" That's just about the highest praise a salad could get.

Crispy Pita

2 pitas, torn into 1-inch pieces

1½ tablespoons extra-virgin olive oil

Heaping ¼ teaspoon garlic powder

Heaping ¼ teaspoon sumac

¼ teaspoon sea salt

Sumac Dressing

1½ tablespoons extra-virgin olive oil

1½ tablespoons fresh lemon juice

¾ teaspoon honey or maple syrup

¼ teaspoon sea salt

¼ teaspoon sumac

For the Salad

6 cups chopped romaine lettuce

1 watermelon radish, halved and thinly sliced

1 medium carrot, very thinly sliced

¼ medium red onion, very thinly sliced

5 soft Medjool dates, pitted and chopped*

¾ cup crumbled feta cheese

⅔ cup Eggplant Yogurt Sauce (page 34)

2 tablespoons water, plus more as needed

Aleppo pepper

Fresh mint leaves, for garnish

**If your dates are not soft, soak them in warm water for 5 to 10 minutes.*

Preheat the oven to 375°F and line a baking sheet with parchment paper.

Make the crispy pita: Place the pita pieces on the baking sheet. Drizzle with the olive oil and sprinkle with the garlic powder, sumac, and salt. Toss to coat and spread evenly on the baking sheet. Bake for 15 to 20 minutes, or until crisp, tossing halfway through.

Make the sumac dressing: In a small lidded jar, combine the olive oil, lemon juice, honey, salt, and sumac. Cover and shake to combine.

Make the salad: Place the romaine, radishes, carrots, and onions in a large bowl. Drizzle with the sumac dressing and toss to coat. Add the dates, half the feta, and half the crispy pita and toss again. Season to taste.

Place the eggplant yogurt sauce in a medium bowl. Stir in the water, adding more as needed to reach a creamy, drizzleable consistency.

Spread a thin layer of the sauce at the bottom of a large, shallow serving bowl. Top with the romaine mixture. Add the remaining feta and crispy pita and lightly toss. Drizzle with more of the sauce, then sprinkle with Aleppo pepper and garnish with mint.

Season to taste and serve with the remaining eggplant yogurt sauce on the side.

SERVES **4** *TO* **6**

VEGAN: Skip the feta or use vegan feta. Use vegan Eggplant Yogurt Sauce (page 34).

GLUTEN-FREE: Use gluten-free pita.

MORE WAYS TO USE

EGGPLANT YOGURT SAUCE

+

On a Mediterranean mezze platter

alongside hummus, cubed feta, and olives. Serve with fresh veggies and pita for dipping!

+

In a creamy eggplant pasta.

Toss the sauce with your favorite short pasta and bursty sautéed cherry tomatoes (or the roasted tomatoes on page 260). Garnish with roughly crumbled feta and fresh mint or parsley.

+

On a grilled halloumi grain bowl

with bulgur, grilled peppers or zucchini, Pickled Onions (page 19), and fresh mint.

In crispy chickpea tacos.

Load up tortillas with a scoop of the sauce, roasted chickpeas, and diced cucumbers and tomatoes. Top with Pickled Onions (page 19) or Jalapeño Radish Pickles (page 88) and fresh cilantro and parsley.

In a smoky summer salad.

Spread a swoosh of the sauce on a serving platter. Top with grilled veggies like eggplant, corn kernels, and green beans. Squeeze lemon juice on top, drizzle with more sauce, and garnish with soft, leafy herbs.

Over herb-packed stuffed peppers.

Make a quick filling by tossing tabbouleh with chickpeas and olives. Load into grilled or roasted pepper halves and drizzle generously with the sauce!

CREAMY CORN SAUCE

In the Midwest, sweet corn season is everything. As soon as corn appears at the markets, it's all I can think about. Even my toddler, Ollie, gets excited for "corn on the bob" season and sits on the back stoop to help me shuck. Though it's tough to beat corn straight off the cob, I'm always experimenting with other ways to use it. This luxe sauce is one of my favorites. It's smooth, creamy, and filled with the corn's natural sweetness. The basic version is wonderful on pasta or in my Sweet Corn Orzotto (page 53). If I'm using it in a Southwest- or Mexican-inspired recipe, I blend in pickled jalapeños and chipotle powder for a smoky, spicy kick.

TIP

This sauce is best made with fresh summer sweet corn. If you want to make it at another time of year, substitute thawed frozen corn kernels for fresh ones. They'll be sweeter and juicier than the out-of-season stuff!

3 ears corn (to yield 2¼ cups kernels), shucked

2 tablespoons plus 1 teaspoon avocado oil

1 teaspoon sea salt

Freshly ground black pepper

¾ cup raw cashews

¼ cup water, plus more as needed

1 tablespoon fresh lemon juice

2 garlic cloves

¼ teaspoon onion powder

For the Enchilada or Nacho Sauce

2 tablespoons pickled jalapeño peppers

¼ teaspoon chipotle powder

YIELD: ABOUT **2** *CUPS*

VEGAN | GLUTEN-FREE

Slice the kernels off the corncobs, then use the back of a chef's knife to scrape off the milky liquid that's left on the cobs.

Heat 1 teaspoon of the avocado oil in a large skillet over medium heat. Add the corn kernels, ½ teaspoon of the salt, and several grinds of pepper. Cook, stirring, for 4 minutes, or until tender and bright yellow.

Transfer the sautéed corn to a high-speed blender and add the remaining 2 tablespoons avocado oil, the milky corn liquid, cashews, water, lemon juice, garlic, onion powder, and the remaining ½ teaspoon salt. Blend until smooth, gradually adding more water as needed to create a smooth, creamy, and pourable sauce. Depending on the starch and moisture content of your corn, you may need up to ½ cup more water to reach a smooth and creamy consistency.

Stop here if making the Sweet Corn Orzotto (page 53). For the Sweet Corn Enchiladas (page 47) or Loaded Corn Nachos (page 51), add the pickled jalapeños and chipotle powder and blend again.

Store in an airtight container in the refrigerator for up to 5 days.

SWEET CORN ENCHILADAS

WITH CREAMY CORN SAUCE

These fresh, summery enchiladas are a corn trifecta! They combine corn tortillas and a charred corn filling with my delicious corn sauce. The sauce is so creamy and flavorful that you really don't need cheese here, so these enchiladas happen to be vegan.

2 ears corn, shucked

1 small white onion, diced

2 jalapeño peppers, stemmed and thinly sliced

1 tablespoon avocado oil, plus more for brushing

1 medium yellow squash, sliced into thin half-moons

1 red bell pepper, stemmed, seeded, and diced

¾ teaspoon sea salt

Freshly ground black pepper

6 ounces extra-firm tofu, patted dry and crumbled

½ teaspoon chipotle powder

1½ cups tomatillo salsa

8 tortillas, warmed (we like a corn and flour blend)

1 cup Creamy Corn Sauce (page 44)

1 avocado, sliced

Fresh cilantro leaves, for garnish

Lime wedges, for serving

Preheat the oven to 400°F and brush a 9×13-inch or similar baking dish with avocado oil.

Char the corn. Heat a large cast-iron skillet over medium-high heat. Add the ears of corn and cook, rotating them as they char, for 7 to 8 minutes, or until charred on all sides. Remove from the pan and, once cool enough to handle, slice the kernels off the corncobs.

Set aside ¼ cup diced white onion, half the jalapeños, and half the corn kernels for topping.

Make the filling. Return the pan to the stove and heat the avocado oil over medium heat. Add the remaining onions and cook for 2 minutes, or until beginning to soften. Add the remaining jalapeños, the yellow squash, bell pepper, salt, and several grinds of pepper. Cook, stirring occasionally, for 3 to 5 minutes, or until the squash is tender but still has a slight bite. Remove from the heat and stir in the tofu, chipotle powder, and remaining corn kernels.

RECIPE CONTINUES

Assemble the enchiladas. Spread a heaping ½ cup of the tomatillo salsa at the bottom of the prepared baking dish. Fill each tortilla with 1 tablespoon of the corn sauce and ⅓ cup of the filling mixture. Roll the tortillas and place seam side down in the baking dish.

Pour the remaining salsa down the middle of the enchiladas, leaving the edges bare. Cover with foil and bake for 15 minutes, then uncover and bake for 10 to 20 minutes, or until the edges of the tortillas are crisp.

Check the consistency of the remaining corn sauce. If it's too thick to pour, add water, 1 tablespoon at a time, as needed to reach a creamy, pourable consistency. Pour the sauce down the middle of the enchiladas and top with the reserved white onion, jalapeños, and corn kernels as well as the avocado and cilantro. Serve with lime wedges.

SERVES **4**

VEGAN

GLUTEN-FREE: Use gluten-free tortillas.

LOADED CORN NACHOS

WITH CREAMY CORN SAUCE

I love making nacho sauces out of vegetables. There's a butternut squash queso in *Love & Lemons Every Day*, and we also have some tasty sweet potato nachos and cauliflower nachos on the blog. But I have to tell you how much I love these corn nachos! Instead of trying to make the corn sauce taste "cheesy," we let the sweet corn flavor really shine through. Load these up with fresh toppings, and you'll find yourself going back for chip after chip.

1 ear corn, shucked

1½ cups Creamy Corn Sauce (page 44)

6 ounces tortilla chips

¼ cup crumbled cotija cheese

½ cup cooked black beans, drained and rinsed (page 320)

1 jalapeño pepper, stemmed and thinly sliced

Chipotle powder

⅓ cup Pickled Onions (page 19)

⅓ cup fresh cilantro leaves

Lime wedges, for serving

Char the corn. Heat a large cast-iron skillet over medium-high heat. Add the ear of corn and cook, rotating it as it chars, for 7 to 8 minutes, or until charred on all sides. Remove from the pan and, once cool enough to handle, slice the kernels off the corncob.

Check the consistency of the corn sauce. If it's too thick to drizzle, add water, 1 tablespoon at a time, as needed to reach a creamy, drizzleable consistency.

Arrange the tortilla chips in a thin layer on a large platter or baking sheet. Evenly drizzle the corn sauce on top, then sprinkle with the cotija cheese followed by the black beans, grilled corn kernels, jalapeños, and pinches of chipotle powder. Top with the pickled onions and cilantro.

Serve with lime wedges.

SERVES **4** *TO* **6**

VEGAN: Skip the cheese.

GLUTEN-FREE

SWEET CORN ORZOTTO

WITH CREAMY CORN SAUCE

Want to make a dish that tastes like risotto with about three hundred fewer stirs? Make this creamy orzotto! You'll simply mix cooked orzo with our creamy corn sauce to create a comforting risotto-like dish. Sautéed corn kernels and Fresno chiles add texture and a little heat, and a handful of fresh basil makes it oh-so-summery. For quick weeknight cooking, I like to make the creamy corn sauce a day or two in advance.

12 ounces orzo pasta

2 tablespoons extra-virgin olive oil, plus more for drizzling

Kernels from 3 ears corn (2¼ cups)

1 Fresno chile, stemmed and thinly sliced (optional)

½ teaspoon sea salt

Freshly ground black pepper

1½ cups Creamy Corn Sauce (page 44), warmed

½ cup water, plus more as needed

1 to 2 tablespoons fresh lemon juice

Red pepper flakes (optional)

Fresh basil leaves, for garnish

Grated pecorino cheese, for serving

Bring a large pot of salted water to a boil. Prepare the orzo according to the package instructions, cooking until al dente. Drain and toss with a drizzle of olive oil to prevent sticking.

Heat 1 tablespoon of the olive oil in a large, deep skillet over medium heat. Add the corn kernels, Fresno chile (if using), salt, and several grinds of pepper. Cook, stirring occasionally, for 2 minutes, or until the corn kernels are bright yellow and the chile is tender. Remove from the heat. Scoop out ½ cup of the corn and chile mixture and set aside.

Add the orzo, corn sauce, water, and the remaining 1 tablespoon olive oil to the corn in the skillet and stir to combine. The orzo should have a creamy, risotto-like texture. If it's too thick, gradually add more water as needed to loosen it. Depending on the starch and moisture content of your corn, you may need up to 1 cup more water to reach a creamy consistency.

Stir in 1 tablespoon lemon juice, then season to taste, adding 1 more tablespoon lemon juice if desired.

Portion onto four plates and top with the reserved sautéed corn and chiles. Sprinkle with red pepper flakes, if desired. Drizzle with olive oil, garnish with basil, and serve with grated pecorino cheese.

SERVES **4**

VEGAN: Skip the cheese.

GLUTEN-FREE: Use gluten-free orzo.

MORE WAYS TO USE

CREAMY CORN SAUCE

On summery flatbreads

topped with grilled corn, scallions, and peppers; feta; and a shower of fresh basil.

In any-veggie tacos.

Fill tortillas with a swoosh of the sauce, then add whatever grilled or roasted veggies you like. Some black beans, avocado, Pickled Onions (page 19), cilantro, and/or cotija cheese would be great here too.

In a double-corn Mexican street corn dip.

Fold grilled corn kernels and scallions into some of the sauce to create a thick, creamy dip with plenty of texture. Garnish with more grilled corn, more scallions, diced jalapeños, and cotija cheese before serving!

Over Southwest stuffed avocados

filled with a black bean and corn salad. Garnish with cilantro and toasted pepitas!

In a creamy corn pasta.

Toss the sauce with your favorite pasta and sautéed veggies, such as zucchini, yellow squash, spinach, and/or cherry tomatoes. Top with fresh basil and Parmesan cheese.

In a shortcut corn chowder.

Sauté sliced onion, celery, and garlic until softened, then add cubed potatoes, corn, and vegetable broth and simmer until the potatoes are tender. Stir in a scoop of the sauce to give the chowder a luxe creamy texture.

In yellow gazpacho.

Blend some of the sauce with yellow tomatoes, yellow bell pepper, cucumber, a splash of white wine vinegar, and a handful of basil to create a refreshing summer soup.

BURSTY CHERRY TOMATO SAUCE

Here's how I shop for cherry tomatoes in the summer: I show up at the farmers market on Saturday mornings with a toddler who can't help but eat a few tomatoes from each pint at my favorite farm stand. Since I don't want anyone else to get shortchanged on their tomatoes, I end up grabbing all those pints and coming home with way too many. I can't say it's a bad problem to have, because it means this bursty cherry tomato sauce has a permanent spot in my summer rotation. A cut above your average marinara, it's super sweet and fresh-tasting, with a touch of miso mixed in for rich, almost buttery flavor.

½ cup extra-virgin olive oil

4 garlic cloves, sliced

½ teaspoon red pepper flakes (optional)

2½ pounds cherry tomatoes (4 pints)

Freshly ground black pepper

3 tablespoons white miso paste

YIELD: ABOUT **4** *CUPS*

VEGAN | GLUTEN-FREE

Heat the olive oil in a large pot or Dutch oven over medium heat. Add the garlic and red pepper flakes, if using, and cook for 1 minute. Add the tomatoes and several grinds of pepper. Cook, stirring occasionally, for 6 to 8 minutes, or until the tomatoes begin to break down and are surrounded by bubbly juices. Add the miso paste and stir to incorporate.

Reduce the heat to medium-low and simmer, uncovered and stirring occasionally, for 10 to 20 minutes, or until the sauce thickens but some tomatoes still retain their shape. Season to taste.

Store in an airtight container in the refrigerator for up to 5 days.

BUCATINI WITH PISTACHIO GREMOLATA

& BURSTY CHERRY TOMATO SAUCE

Paired with a glass of white wine and a Michigan sunset, this simple, elegant pasta might be my ideal summer meal. You could technically use any noodle here, but I love the long, chewy bucatini in the glossy sauce. I top it off with a quick pistachio gremolata, which adds a hit of fresh, garlicky flavor to this already delicious dish.

1 recipe Bursty Cherry Tomato Sauce (page 56)

12 ounces bucatini pasta

Pistachio Gremolata

½ cup finely chopped fresh parsley

½ cup shelled raw pistachios, toasted and crushed

1 tablespoon lemon zest

1 garlic clove, grated

¼ teaspoon sea salt

½ cup extra-virgin olive oil

Prepare the bursty cherry tomato sauce according to the recipe. If you've made the sauce ahead of time, warm it in a Dutch oven or large skillet.

Meanwhile, make the pistachio gremolata: In a medium bowl, stir together the parsley, pistachios, lemon zest, garlic, and salt. Drizzle in the olive oil and mix until combined.

Bring a large pot of salted water to a boil. Prepare the pasta according to the package instructions, cooking until al dente. Use tongs to transfer it from the pot to the Dutch oven or skillet with the sauce. Toss to coat and season to taste.

Portion into bowls, top with the pistachio gremolata, and serve.

SERVES **4** | **VEGAN** | **GLUTEN-FREE:** Use gluten-free pasta.

CHEESY BAKED POLENTA

WITH BURSTY CHERRY TOMATO SAUCE

This recipe is perfect for those few summer sweater-weather days—the ones in late August that give you a break from the heat and make it okay to turn on the oven and bake something oozy and comforting. Creamy polenta is topped with our bursty cherry tomato sauce and smothered in cheese. Serve it alongside a green salad tossed with my lemon vinaigrette (page 282) for a simple, satisfying meal.

Extra-virgin olive oil, for brushing

3 cups water, plus more as needed

½ teaspoon sea salt

1 cup quick-cooking polenta

2 cups Bursty Cherry Tomato Sauce (page 56)

1½ cups grated fontina cheese

Red pepper flakes

Fresh basil leaves, for garnish

Preheat the oven to 425°F and brush an 8×11-inch or similar baking dish with olive oil.

Bring the water and salt to a boil in a medium pot. Gradually add the polenta, whisking continuously. Cook, whisking often, for 5 minutes, or until the polenta is tender, thick, and creamy. Reduce the heat to low as needed to prevent the polenta from sputtering as it thickens. The cooking times of different brands of polenta can vary. If your polenta is not tender after 5 minutes, add water as needed and continue cooking until tender, thick, and creamy.

Remove from the heat. Spread the polenta evenly in the prepared baking dish. Set aside for 5 minutes to cool, then top with the cherry tomato sauce, leaving a ½-inch border around the edges. Sprinkle the cheese evenly on top.

Bake for 25 to 30 minutes, or until the cheese is browned and bubbling. Let cool for 15 minutes, then sprinkle with red pepper flakes, garnish with basil, and serve.

SERVES **4**

GLUTEN-FREE

TOMATO COCONUT CURRY

WITH BURSTY CHERRY TOMATO SAUCE

I love a recipe that lets you cook once and eat twice. Once you've made the baked polenta on the prior page, use up the leftover bursty cherry tomato sauce in this easy curry. Don't worry—you won't be eating the same flavors two nights in a row. Quickly simmered with coconut milk, ginger, curry powder, and jalapeño, the sauce transforms into an aromatic curry that tastes like it's been bubbling away all day. It also reheats and freezes well, so it's perfect for meal prep.

1 tablespoon coconut oil

½ medium yellow onion, chopped

½ to 1 jalapeño pepper, stemmed and chopped

1 (1-inch) piece fresh ginger, peeled and cut into thin matchsticks

¼ teaspoon sea salt

Heaping ½ teaspoon curry powder

2 cups Bursty Cherry Tomato Sauce (page 56)

1 (13.5-ounce) can full-fat coconut milk

8 ounces paneer cheese, cut into ½-inch cubes

2 cups small cauliflower florets

¾ cup fresh cilantro, stems chopped, leaves reserved

1 teaspoon lime zest

1½ teaspoons fresh lime juice

Cooked rice (page 320), for serving

Naan, for serving

Heat the coconut oil in a medium pot or Dutch oven over medium heat. Add the onions, jalapeños, ginger, and salt and cook, stirring occasionally, for 2 minutes. Add the curry powder and cook, stirring, for 3 minutes, or until the onion is softened.

Add the cherry tomato sauce, coconut milk, paneer, and cauliflower. Stir to combine and reduce the heat to low. Simmer, uncovered, for 15 minutes. Add the cilantro stems and lime zest and simmer for 3 more minutes, or until the cauliflower is tender but still has a slight bite.

Stir in the lime juice and half the cilantro leaves. Season to taste and serve with rice, naan, and the remaining cilantro leaves for garnish.

SERVES **4**

VEGAN: Replace the paneer with extra-firm tofu.

GLUTEN-FREE: Serve with gluten-free naan or skip the naan.

MORE WAYS TO USE

BURSTY CHERRY TOMATO SAUCE

On a mouthwatering burrata platter.

Spoon the sauce over burrata cheese and garnish with fresh basil. Serve with grilled bread for scooping up the sauce and cheese.

In a comforting gnocchi dish.

Toss the sauce with cooked gnocchi. Serve topped with fresh basil or parsley and dollops of ricotta cheese.

In a cherry tomato soup.

Blend the sauce with a little vegetable broth to create the best tomato soup you've ever tasted.

In fresh tomato shakshuka.

Stir a little harissa into the sauce and bring it to a simmer in a lidded skillet. Create wells in the sauce and crack in eggs. Cover and cook until the egg whites are set.

As a base for ratatouille.

Fold roasted eggplant, zucchini, peppers, and onions into the sauce and add a splash of sherry vinegar. Simmer to develop the flavors, then serve topped with fresh basil and a big drizzle of olive oil.

GUIDE TO GREEN SAUCES

If you have soft, leafy herbs on hand, you're just minutes away from having a vibrant green sauce to drizzle over anything and everything. Enjoy these as dipping sauces and salad dressings, on pastas, grain bowls, sandwiches, and more!

CILANTRO

CITRUS SERRANO SAUCE

2 serrano peppers, stemmed and chopped
1 cup cilantro
2 scallions, roughly chopped
1 garlic clove
½ cup avocado oil
¼ cup orange juice
1 tablespoon lime juice
2 teaspoons honey or maple syrup
¼ teaspoon sea salt

Blend.

→ **Avocado Serrano Salsa**
Add 4 roasted tomatillos, ½ avocado, and an extra pinch of salt.

SHARED HERBS

GREEN GODDESS

2 cups mixed leafy herbs
1 cup whole milk Greek yogurt
3 tablespoons olive oil
2 tablespoons lemon juice
1 garlic clove
½ teaspoon sea salt

Pulse in a food processor.

↓ **Tahini Green Goddess**
Replace the yogurt with ½ cup tahini. Add an extra 1 tablespoon lemon juice, 1 teaspoon honey or maple syrup, and ¼ cup water, or more as needed.

BASIL

BASIL PESTO

2 cups basil leaves
½ cup toasted pine nuts
1½ tablespoons lemon juice
1 small garlic clove
¼ teaspoon sea salt
⅓ cup olive oil

Pulse in a food processor.

→ **Mint Pesto**
Replace half the basil with mint.

↓ **Minty Pea Pesto**
Replace the pine nuts with thawed frozen peas.

MINT

COCONUT MINT SAUCE

2 cups cilantro
2 cups mint leaves
½ cup unsweetened coconut yogurt
2 tablespoons lime juice
2 teaspoons avocado oil
2 teaspoons grated fresh ginger
1 small garlic clove
1 teaspoon sugar
½ teaspoon sea salt

Pulse in a food processor.

Coconut Curry Mint Sauce
Replace the lime juice with lemon juice. Add ½ teaspoon curry powder.

PARSLEY

CHIMICHURRI

1 cup cilantro
1 cup parsley
⅔ cup olive oil
¼ cup white wine vinegar
2 garlic cloves
½ teaspoon dried oregano
½ teaspoon red pepper flakes
½ teaspoon sea salt
½ teaspoon smoked paprika

Pulse in a food processor.

Chimichurri Aioli
Mix 3 tablespoons chimichurri into 1 cup mayo.

Zucchini Chimichurri
Pulse in 1 medium zucchini.

ITALIAN SALSA VERDE

¾ cup olive oil
1 garlic clove, grated
1 cup parsley, finely chopped
½ cup basil leaves, finely chopped
2 tablespoons chopped capers
1 tablespoon lemon juice
½ teaspoon red pepper flakes
Pinch of sea salt

Stir together.

Pepperoncini Italian Salsa Verde
Replace the capers with ¼ cup finely chopped pepperoncini. Increase the salt to ¼ teaspoon.

TARRAGON

CREAMY TARRAGON DILL SAUCE

½ cup mayonnaise
½ cup whole milk Greek yogurt
1 tablespoon lemon juice
1 teaspoon Dijon mustard
¼ teaspoon ground turmeric
3 tablespoons finely chopped tarragon
2 tablespoons finely chopped chives
2 tablespoons finely chopped dill

Stir together, adding water as needed.

Tarragon Tzatziki
Skip the turmeric. Increase the yogurt to 1 cup. Add ½ cup grated cucumber, 1 tablespoon olive oil, 2 grated garlic cloves, and ¼ teaspoon salt.

DILL

GREEN RANCH

1½ cups raw cashews
¾ cup water, plus more as needed
¼ cup distilled white vinegar
1 teaspoon sea salt
¾ teaspoon garlic powder
¾ teaspoon onion powder
Freshly ground black pepper
⅓ cup chopped chives
⅓ cup chopped dill

Blend.

Spicy Green Ranch
Cut the vinegar and salt in half. Add ½ cup pickled jalapeños.

Super Green Ranch
Add 4 cups fresh spinach.

AN ACTUALLY GOOD WEDGE SALAD

WITH GREEN RANCH

After my co-author, Phoebe, and I created our Guide to Green Sauces, we picked a few of our favorites to pair with full recipes. We immediately thought this green ranch sounded fun . . . and for contrast, we decided to pair it with a dish we both find, well . . . un-fun—the wedge salad. (Sorry, wedge lovers!) Our issue with a traditional wedge is that the dressing and ingredients slide off its peak, leaving a bunch of bland iceberg in the middle. So here, we cut the lettuce into smaller pieces with flatter surfaces so that our punchy sauce and crispy toppings have nowhere to go. Call us wedge converts—this saucy, crunchy, herby, and refreshing salad is one of our new favorites.

Green Ranch

1½ cups raw cashews
¾ cup water, plus more as needed
¼ cup distilled white vinegar
1 teaspoon sea salt
¾ teaspoon garlic powder
¾ teaspoon onion powder
Freshly ground black pepper
⅓ cup chopped fresh chives
⅓ cup chopped fresh dill

For the Salad

1 head iceberg lettuce
Sea salt and freshly ground black pepper
4 red radishes, thinly sliced
1 Persian cucumber, thinly sliced
2 tablespoons toasted sunflower seeds
1 tablespoon chopped fresh chives
1 tablespoon chopped fresh dill
Lemon wedges, for serving

Make the green ranch: In a high-speed blender, place the cashews, water, vinegar, salt, garlic powder, onion powder, and several grinds of pepper. Blend until smooth, then add the chives and dill and blend until the sauce is smooth with green flecks. Chill in the refrigerator until ready to serve.

Make the salad: Place the lettuce upright on a cutting board and slice it into four equal slabs. Place each slab cut side down on the cutting board and halve it lengthwise from the root end to the top. Trim off and discard any tough core pieces, leaving just enough core to keep the wedges intact.

Check the consistency of the green ranch. If it's too thick to drizzle, add water, 1 tablespoon at a time, as needed to thin it to a thick drizzleable consistency. Spread a thin layer of the ranch on a large serving platter.

Arrange the lettuce evenly over the ranch, keeping the wedges intact. Season with salt and spoon on more of the ranch. Top with the radishes and cucumbers, then drizzle with more ranch and season with several grinds of pepper. Sprinkle with the sunflower seeds, chives, and dill and serve with lemon wedges.

SERVES **8** | VEGAN | GLUTEN-FREE

GRILLED BROCCOLI

WITH PEPPERONCINI ITALIAN SALSA VERDE

While Phoebe and I were brainstorming green sauce ideas, we first thought of every type of classic herb sauce, then came up with fun twists. At one point, when we got stuck, I opened my fridge looking for condiment inspiration and shouted, "Pepperoncini!" These little pickled peppers turned out to be the perfect fun ingredient to punch up a classic Italian salsa verde. This sauce is delicious spooned over any grilled or roasted vegetable, but we especially love it over grilled broccoli and ricotta for a simple, showstopping side dish.

Pepperoncini Italian Salsa Verde

¾ cup extra-virgin olive oil

1 garlic clove, grated

1 cup fresh parsley, finely chopped

½ cup fresh basil leaves, finely chopped

¼ cup finely chopped pepperoncini (about 4)

1 tablespoon fresh lemon juice

½ teaspoon red pepper flakes

¼ teaspoon sea salt

Lemon Ricotta

1 cup whole milk ricotta cheese

2 teaspoons fresh lemon juice

¼ teaspoon sea salt

For the Broccoli

1 pound broccoli (about 2 medium heads)

2 tablespoons extra-virgin olive oil

¼ teaspoon sea salt

Freshly ground black pepper

Lemon zest, for garnish

Make the pepperoncini Italian salsa verde: In a medium bowl, stir together the olive oil and garlic. Add the parsley, basil, pepperoncini, lemon juice, red pepper flakes, and salt and stir until well combined.

Make the lemon ricotta: In another medium bowl, stir together the ricotta, lemon juice, and salt.

Grill the broccoli: Cut the broccoli into large 4-inch florets. Trim the long sides to create flat edges that will make direct contact with the grill grates.

Preheat a grill or grill pan to medium-high heat. In a large bowl, toss the broccoli with the olive oil, salt, and several grinds of pepper, using your hands to make sure the tops of the broccoli florets are well oiled.

Place the broccoli on the grill and tent with foil. Grill for 5 to 8 minutes on the first side, or until char marks form. Flip, tent with foil again, and grill for 3 to 6 minutes on the second side, or until the broccoli is tender and well charred. If it's charring faster than it's becoming tender, reduce the heat to low.

Spread the ricotta on a large serving platter. Top with the grilled broccoli and spoon the salsa verde on top. Season to taste, garnish with lemon zest, and serve.

SERVES **4** *AS A SIDE*

VEGAN: Replace the ricotta cheese with whipped tofu (page 322).

GLUTEN-FREE

MAKE THIS RECIPE IN THE OVEN

Arrange the veggies in a single layer on two baking sheets lined with parchment paper. Bake at 425°F for 20 minutes, or until golden brown and crisp.

AIR FRYER FRITTO MISTO

WITH CREAMY TARRAGON DILL SAUCE

When you order fritto misto at a restaurant (hopefully a seaside one in Southern Italy), you'll likely get a mix of seafood that's been dipped in a light batter and fried until crisp. "Mixed fry" is the literal translation, so we made a "mixed air fry" version to enjoy at home—using meaty mushrooms, briny artichokes, and slender green beans instead of fish. Don't skip the creamy, tangy tarragon sauce for dipping!

Creamy Tarragon Dill Sauce

½ cup mayonnaise

½ cup whole milk Greek yogurt

1 tablespoon fresh lemon juice

1 teaspoon Dijon mustard

¼ teaspoon ground turmeric

3 tablespoons finely chopped fresh tarragon

2 tablespoons finely chopped fresh chives

2 tablespoons finely chopped fresh dill

For the Fritto Misto

1½ cups panko bread crumbs

¾ teaspoon sea salt

½ teaspoon garlic powder

½ teaspoon onion powder

2 large eggs

1 (14-ounce) can artichoke hearts, drained, patted dry, and halved lengthwise

4 ounces oyster mushrooms

2 ounces fresh green beans, trimmed

Extra-virgin olive oil, for drizzling

Lemon wedges, for serving

Make the creamy tarragon dill sauce: In a medium bowl, stir together the mayonnaise, yogurt, lemon juice, mustard, and turmeric. Add the tarragon, chives, and dill and stir to combine. The sauce should have a creamy, dollopable consistency. If it's too thick, add water, 1 tablespoon at a time, as needed to loosen it. Season to taste and chill in the refrigerator until ready to serve.

Make the fritto misto: On a rimmed tray, mix together the panko, salt, garlic powder, and onion powder. In a shallow bowl, beat the eggs.

Dip each artichoke half, mushroom, and green bean into the egg, then coat in the panko mixture. Place on a large plate or baking sheet and drizzle with olive oil.

Preheat the air fryer to 400°F. Working in batches if necessary, arrange the veggies in a single layer in the air fryer basket, leaving a little space around each one. Air fry for 8 to 12 minutes, or until golden brown and crisp.

Season to taste and serve with lemon wedges and creamy tarragon dill sauce for dipping.

SERVES **4** *AS AN APPETIZER*

GLUTEN-FREE: Use gluten-free panko.

SHEET PAN QUESADILLAS

WITH CITRUS SERRANO SAUCE

So much of this book is about contrast—contrasting textures, flavors, and even colors. It's contrast that makes a dish exciting to eat—something crispy with something creamy, something spicy with something cooling, something deeply charred with something bright. This recipe is a prime example. The vibrant serrano sauce perfectly balances the quesadillas, which are baked until the cheese around the edges is as crisp and browned as can be. The combination is absolutely irresistible.

1 poblano pepper

1 red bell pepper

8 (6-inch) flour tortillas, warmed

1 heaping cup grated Mexican cheese blend

2 scallions, chopped

½ cup cooked black beans, drained and rinsed (page 320)

Sea salt

4 ounces Oaxaca cheese, torn into thin strips

Avocado oil spray

Citrus Serrano Sauce

2 serrano peppers, stemmed and chopped

1 cup fresh cilantro

2 scallions, roughly chopped

1 garlic clove

½ cup avocado oil

¼ cup fresh orange juice

1 tablespoon fresh lime juice

2 teaspoons honey or maple syrup

¼ teaspoon sea salt

Heat a dry cast-iron skillet over medium-high heat. Add the poblano and red bell pepper and cook, rotating the peppers as they char, for 10 to 12 minutes, or until charred on all sides.

Allow the peppers to cool slightly, then peel away any large, loose pieces of charred skin. Remove the stems, seeds, and membranes, then slice into thin strips.

Meanwhile, make the citrus serrano sauce: In a blender, place the serranos, cilantro, scallions, garlic, avocado oil, orange juice, lime juice, honey, and salt. Blend until smooth and season to taste.

Preheat the oven to 425°F and line a large baking sheet with parchment paper.

Place one of the tortillas on the baking sheet. Sprinkle a little of the Mexican cheese blend over one side of the tortilla and top with a few pepper strips, some of the scallions, and black beans. Sprinkle with salt and top with some of the Oaxaca cheese. Fold the other side of the tortilla over the fillings to close. Repeat with the remaining tortillas and spread the quesadillas evenly on the baking sheet. Spray with avocado oil spray.

Bake for 10 to 15 minutes, or until the edges of the tortillas are crisp. Flip and bake for another 10 to 15 minutes, or until the tortillas are crisp and the edges of the melted cheese are crispy and browned.

Remove from the oven and serve with the citrus serrano sauce.

SERVES **4**

VEGAN: Use vegan cheese shreds.

GLUTEN-FREE: Use gluten-free tortillas.

CHAPTER 2

CHILI CRISP
JALAPEÑO RADISH PICKLES
HARISSA
GIARDINIERA
SPICY TURMERIC PASTE

SPICY

After living in Austin for twenty years, I adore spice. Adding a little heat is one of my favorite ways to bring a dish to life, whether through a pickled pepper or a chile-spiked sauce. Spice skeptics, don't worry—I've included tips and ranges so that you can spice all these recipes to your level.

CHILI CRISP

Chili crisp first entered my kitchen in the lockdown of 2020, when cooking was all about hardworking pantry ingredients. If it hasn't entered yours yet, get ready—once you start cooking with this Chinese condiment, you won't stop. It consists of a chile-infused oil packed with crunchy mix-ins like fried or dehydrated garlic and shallots, fermented soybeans, Sichuan peppercorns, and/or sesame seeds. A spoonful or two will add a burst of savory, spicy, umami flavor to just about any dish. Simple pasta? Add chili crisp. Avocado toast? More chili crisp, please. Ice cream? Okay, I haven't actually done that one, but I'm about to head to the kitchen to try it. You can find chili crisp in many supermarkets, Asian grocery stores, or online. If you need a rec, my favorite brand is Fly By Jing!

SPICY EGGS & YOGURT

WITH CHILI CRISP

This is my favorite breakfast to make on a weekday morning. Yes, I said it—weekday. It would be great for a weekend brunch too, but it's so simple that it's weekday-possible, even if you have a child running around in a superhero cape, refusing to finish his breakfast and get dressed for school. It's based on the Turkish egg dish çilbir, which is often made with an Aleppo pepper butter or olive oil sauce. Instead of using a homemade sauce here, I give this recipe an Asian spin by topping it with store-bought chili crisp. Just poach the eggs, season the yogurt (or prep the yogurt in advance), drizzle with chili crisp, and dig in!

4 large eggs

1 tablespoon white wine vinegar

1 cup thick whole milk Greek yogurt (we like Fage or Chobani)

1 garlic clove, grated

1 teaspoon fresh lemon juice

¼ teaspoon sea salt

1 scallion, chopped

Chili crisp, for drizzling

Fresh cilantro leaves, for garnish

Sesame seeds, for garnish

Flaky sea salt

Pita, for serving

Poach the eggs. Crack the eggs into four separate small bowls or ramekins. Bring a medium pot of water to a gentle boil. Add the vinegar and stir the water so that it moves in a circular motion. Gently drop the eggs into the water, give the water another gentle stir, and cook for 3½ to 4 minutes. Use a slotted spoon to scoop the eggs out of the water.

In a medium bowl, stir together the yogurt, garlic, lemon juice, and salt.

Divide the yogurt mixture between two plates or shallow bowls and spread it into a thick swoosh. Top each plate with two poached eggs and sprinkle with the scallions. Drizzle with chili crisp and garnish with cilantro and sesame seeds.

Sprinkle with flaky sea salt and serve with pita.

SERVES **2**

GLUTEN-FREE: Serve with gluten-free pita.

BOK CHOY & DUMPLINGS IN COCONUT BROTH

WITH CHILI CRISP

A drizzle of chili crisp and a couple of sheet pans do the hard work in this recipe. Store-bought dumplings, mushrooms, and bok choy all roast in the oven. While they bake, you'll quickly simmer the zesty coconut broth on the stove. Just pour the broth over the roasted veggies and dumplings and top with chili crisp for a flavor-packed weeknight meal.

1 pound refrigerated or frozen vegetable dumplings

8 ounces shiitake mushrooms, sliced if large, left whole if small

4 baby bok choy (8 ounces), quartered or cut into long strips

Avocado oil, for drizzling

Sea salt

½ cup frozen shelled edamame, thawed

Chili crisp, for serving

Fresh cilantro, for garnish

Coconut Broth

1 (13.5-ounce) can full-fat coconut milk

½ cup water

Zest of 1 lime

1 tablespoon grated fresh ginger

1 garlic clove, grated

2 teaspoons tamari, plus more for serving

¼ teaspoon sea salt

1 tablespoon fresh lime juice

Preheat the oven to 425°F and line two baking sheets with parchment paper.

Place the dumplings on one side of one of the baking sheets and the mushrooms on the other side. Place the bok choy on the second baking sheet. Drizzle all three with avocado oil and sprinkle the mushrooms and bok choy with salt. Toss to coat and spread evenly on the baking sheets.

Roast the dumplings and mushrooms for 10 to 25 minutes, or until the dumplings are tender and warmed through and the mushrooms are tender and browned around the edges. If the dumplings are ready first, remove them from the baking sheet and continue roasting the mushrooms. Roast the bok choy for 10 to 12 minutes, or until the stems are crisp-tender and the leaves are wilted.

Meanwhile, make the coconut broth: Heat the coconut milk, water, lime zest, ginger, garlic, tamari, and salt in a medium saucepan over medium heat. Simmer, uncovered, for 10 minutes. Stir in the lime juice.

Divide the dumplings, mushrooms, bok choy, and edamame among four bowls. Pour in enough broth to submerge the dumplings and vegetables halfway. Top the bowls with chili crisp and garnish with cilantro. Serve with more chili crisp and tamari.

SERVES **4**

VEGAN: Use vegan dumplings.

SMASHED CUCUMBER & CRISPY RICE BOWLS

WITH CHILI CRISP

Everyone knows that the best way to use leftover rice is to make fried rice. But if you need a second way to use it (and if you have it in your fridge as often as I do, you do), the recipe for these crispy rice bowls belongs in your back pocket. I cook the leftover rice in a hot skillet—no stirring!—until it's beautifully golden and crisp underneath. Then, I top it with tangy marinated cucumbers, avocado, and silken tofu. I LOVE the combination of the creamy avocado and tofu with the crunchy cucumbers and rice. A few spoonfuls of spicy, savory chili crisp tie it all together.

Smashed Cucumbers

5 Persian cucumbers

½ to 1 Fresno chile, stemmed, halved lengthwise, and very thinly sliced

3 tablespoons rice vinegar

2 tablespoons tamari

1 teaspoon toasted sesame oil

½ teaspoon cane sugar

½ teaspoon grated fresh ginger

¼ teaspoon sea salt

Crispy Rice Bowls

1 tablespoon avocado oil

3 cups leftover cooked rice (page 320)

12 ounces silken tofu, drained and cubed

1 avocado, diced

Chili crisp, for drizzling

2 scallions, chopped, for garnish

⅓ cup fresh mint leaves, for garnish

Sesame seeds, for garnish

Microgreens, for garnish (optional)

Make the smashed cucumbers: Slice the cucumbers in half lengthwise, then crosswise into 1- to 2-inch pieces. Lay the pieces cut side down on a cutting board and use the flat side of a chef's knife to press down on them until they break apart.

Place the cucumbers in a large bowl. Add the Fresno chile, rice vinegar, tamari, sesame oil, sugar, ginger, and salt and toss to combine. Chill in the refrigerator for 15 to 20 minutes to allow the cucumbers to release some of their water.

Make the crispy rice bowls: Heat the avocado oil in a large nonstick skillet over medium-high heat. Add the rice and use a spatula to press it into an even layer at the bottom of the pan. Cook without stirring for 6 to 8 minutes, or until lightly golden and crisp underneath.

Divide the rice among four shallow bowls, placing it crispy side up. Top with the smashed cucumbers, tofu, and avocado. Spoon any remaining juices at the bottom of the cucumber bowl over the rice, then drizzle with chili crisp. Garnish with the scallions, mint, sesame seeds, and microgreens, if using, and serve.

SERVES **4** | **VEGAN** | **GLUTEN-FREE:** Use certified gluten-free tamari.

MORE WAYS TO USE

CHILI CRISP

On a spicy sheet pan dinner.

Toss cubed high-protein tofu and trimmed green beans with chili crisp and a little tamari. Roast until browned and serve over rice.

In a speedy pantry pasta.

Toss chili crisp with your favorite pasta, a pat of butter, and freshly grated Parmesan cheese. Add pasta water as needed to coat the pasta in a glossy sauce.

On soups and stews.

Swirl chili crisp into any Asian-inspired soup, like a miso soup, ramen, or the kimchi noodle soup on page 279.

In a savory salad dressing.

Mix together chili crisp, a little honey, rice vinegar, and avocado oil to create an irresistible dressing. Drizzle over everything—I especially love this one on a slaw made with shredded cabbage, bok choy, scallions, and thinly sliced bell peppers!

On spring-y soba.

Toss cooked soba noodles, blanched asparagus, and snap peas with the sticky peanut sauce on page 153. Top with scallions, baked tofu (page 321 or store-bought), and a spoonful of chili crisp.

On a crunchy celery stir-fry

made by cooking chopped celery, scallions, and bell peppers over medium-high heat until crisp-tender. Feel free to add a protein of your choice!

JALAPEÑO RADISH PICKLES

When I started working on this book, these pickles were one of the first condiments that came to mind. My friend Kelsey and I were having a conversation about what we'd make for a camping trip. Of course, we weren't actually going to camp—but we thought we could pitch a tent in the backyard to entertain Ollie. That led us to dreaming up a glamping menu: homemade tortillas cooked in cast iron over the fire, from-scratch beans, and the easiest part—a crunchy, spicy pickle that I could make ahead to elevate everything. Our little camp never happened, but lucky for us, the pickles did! They really have it all—they're spicy (hence their inclusion in this chapter), but they're also crunchy and tangy, adding an explosion of flavor to whatever you put them on.

TIP

Make your pickles extra-colorful by using a mix of different types of radishes! Green, pink, and purple daikon; watermelon radishes; and red radishes are all great here.

2½ cups very thinly sliced jalapeño peppers (about 8)

1½ cups thin radish half-moons

2 garlic cloves, smashed

¼ cup cane sugar

2 teaspoons sea salt

1 cup rice vinegar

1 cup water, plus more as needed

YIELD: ABOUT **4** *CUPS PICKLES*

VEGAN | GLUTEN-FREE

In a large bowl, toss together the jalapeños and radishes. Evenly divide between two 16-ounce or similar-size lidded jars. Add a garlic clove to each jar.

Evenly divide the sugar, salt, rice vinegar, and water between the jars. Cover and shake to combine. Uncover and check that the vegetables are submerged in the brine, pushing them down and adding more water as needed to fully submerge them. Cover and chill in the refrigerator for at least 1 hour before using.

Store in the refrigerator for up to 2 weeks.

SMOKY POTATO TACOS

WITH JALAPEÑO RADISH PICKLES

The first time I made these tacos, I had leftover jalapeño radish pickles in my fridge, a bowl of potatoes on my countertop . . . and not much else. I was five seconds away from ordering takeout when I thought—potato tacos! I wanted the potatoes to be crispy, so I came up with a shortcut for smashed potatoes: I roasted chunks directly on the pan (no parboiling necessary), then smashed them down and kept roasting until they were super crisp. I stuffed them into tortillas with crema and a pile of pickles, and my husband, Jack, raved, "These are my new favorite tacos!" I'm obsessed with them too, especially because the sheet pan does most of the work, leaving very few dishes to wash after dinner!

Smoky Potatoes

2 pounds small Yukon Gold or yellow potatoes, cut into 2-inch chunks

2 tablespoons extra-virgin olive oil

1 teaspoon garlic powder

1 teaspoon onion powder

1 teaspoon smoked paprika

½ teaspoon sea salt

Freshly ground black pepper

Crema

⅔ cup whole milk Greek yogurt

3 tablespoons mayonnaise

1 tablespoon fresh lime juice

Heaping ¼ teaspoon onion powder

¼ teaspoon garlic powder

⅛ teaspoon sea salt

For the Tacos

8 tortillas, warmed

1 cup Jalapeño Radish Pickles (page 88)

½ cup fresh cilantro leaves

Lime wedges, for serving

Preheat the oven to 450°F and line a baking sheet with parchment paper.

Make the smoky potatoes: Place the potatoes on the baking sheet. Drizzle with the olive oil and sprinkle with the garlic powder, onion powder, ½ teaspoon of the smoked paprika, the salt, and several grinds of pepper. Toss to coat and spread evenly on the baking sheet. Roast for 30 minutes, or until tender.

Remove from the oven. Use the back of a measuring cup to smash the potatoes until about ¼ inch thick. Return to the oven and roast for another 20 to 30 minutes, or until deeply golden brown and crisp underneath. Flip and roast for 5 to 10 more minutes, or until crisp on both sides.

Meanwhile, make the crema: In a medium bowl, stir together the yogurt, mayonnaise, lime juice, onion powder, garlic powder, and salt. Season to taste.

Remove the potatoes from the oven and transfer to a large bowl. While still warm, sprinkle with the remaining ½ teaspoon smoked paprika and toss to coat.

Assemble the tacos: Fill the tortillas with the crema, potatoes, jalapeño radish pickles, and cilantro. Serve with lime wedges.

SERVES **4**

VEGAN: Make the crema vegan by replacing the Greek yogurt with ¾ cup blended silken tofu. Use vegan mayo. Omit the salt and season to taste.

GLUTEN-FREE: Use gluten-free tortillas.

COLD GINGER SESAME UDON

WITH JALAPEÑO RADISH PICKLES

I fell in love with cold udon on the second night of our first trip to Tokyo, in a fog of jet lag, with some local friends who had ordered for the group. The big, chewy noodles were served in a bright, refreshing dashi. They were substantial yet incredibly light and totally fun. Since then, I've kept cold udon in my noodle rotation at home. No version I've made brings that fun feeling quite like this recipe. I toss the slurpable noodles in a sweet, tangy, nutty dressing, and I load them up with a heap of jalapeño radish pickles for heat and crunch. Complete your bowl with a jammy egg, or sub baked tofu to make these noodles vegan.

- 3 tablespoons tamari, plus more for serving
- 2 tablespoons fresh lime juice
- 1 tablespoon toasted sesame oil
- 1½ teaspoons grated fresh ginger
- ¾ cup Jalapeño Radish Pickles (page 88), plus 2 tablespoons brine
- 4 small baby bok choy, leaves separated
- 1¾ pounds jumbo udon noodles
- 4 scallions, thinly sliced
- 4 soft-boiled eggs (page 321), halved lengthwise
- 1 sheet nori, cut into thin strips
- Sesame seeds, for garnish

In a large bowl, stir together the tamari, lime juice, sesame oil, ginger, and 2 tablespoons jalapeño radish pickle brine.

Bring a large pot of water to a boil and set a large bowl of ice water nearby. Drop the bok choy into the boiling water and blanch for 1 minute, or until tender but still bright green. Use a spider or tongs to scoop the bok choy out of the boiling water and into the ice water. Chill for 1 minute, then drain and pat dry with a kitchen towel.

Refill the bowl of ice water and set it near the boiling water. Boil the udon noodles for 1 minute 30 seconds, or for the time listed on the package instructions, then transfer to the ice water and stir until chilled. Drain.

Add the noodles and bok choy to the bowl with the dressing and toss to combine. Divide among four serving bowls, drizzling any dressing left at the bottom of the mixing bowl over the noodles. Top with the scallions, jalapeño radish pickles, eggs, and nori. Garnish with sesame seeds and serve with tamari for seasoning the eggs.

SERVES **4**

VEGAN: Replace the eggs with baked tofu (page 321 or store-bought).

GLUTEN-FREE: Use certified gluten-free tamari and rice noodles instead of jumbo udon.

AVOCADO & CITRUS "CRUDO" TOSTADAS

WITH JALAPEÑO RADISH PICKLES

At my grocery store, tostada shells only come in packs of about 500. I used to have trouble using one up, but once I started making these sweet and spicy tostadas, that problem disappeared. Now I keep getting new packs to make more! The topping here is inspired by a citrusy seafood crudo, but I nix the fish and just use juicy citrus segments instead. The jalapeño radish pickles add extra crunch, acidity, and the perfect kick of heat. I love to serve these as an appetizer, but you could just as easily enjoy them for a refreshing no-cook meal.

Citrus "Crudo"

1 grapefruit

3 mandarin oranges

¼ medium white onion, thinly sliced

1 tablespoon fresh lime juice

1 tablespoon tamari

1 teaspoon toasted sesame oil

For the Tostadas

2 avocados

Pinch of sea salt

4 tostada shells

½ cup Jalapeño Radish Pickles (page 88)

Sesame seeds or Sesame Nori Crisp (page 140), for garnish

Fresh cilantro leaves, for garnish

Flaky sea salt

Make the citrus crudo: Cut the grapefruit in half crosswise. Use a paring knife to loosen the fruit segments, cutting along all three sides of each segment. Use a spoon to scoop out the fruit. Transfer to a large bowl.

Peel the mandarins, cutting away any excess pith. Cut each one in half crosswise, then separate the segments.

Add the mandarin segments, onion, lime juice, tamari, and sesame oil to the bowl with the grapefruit. Toss to combine.

Assemble the tostadas: In a medium bowl, mash the avocados with the salt. Spread onto the tostada shells. Evenly divide the citrus crudo among the tostadas, leaving any excess liquid behind in the bowl. Top with the jalapeño radish pickles and garnish with sesame seeds and cilantro. Sprinkle with flaky sea salt and serve.

SERVES **2** *AS A MAIN OR* **4** *AS AN APPETIZER*

VEGAN

GLUTEN-FREE: Use certified gluten-free tamari.

MORE WAYS TO USE

JALAPEÑO RADISH PICKLES

In a banh mi bowl

with the turmeric baked tofu on page 121, cooked rice (page 320), and cilantro. Serve with the spicy mayo on page 145.

In fresh spring rolls.

Use jalapeño radish pickles instead of the pickled ginger and radishes in the Shiso Spring Rolls on page 231.

On a boring veggie burger.

Boring no more!

In a colorful corn salad.

Toss grilled corn kernels with a quick dressing made from olive oil and jalapeño radish pickle brine. Add a big scoop of the pickles, lime zest, scallions, cilantro, and crumbled feta. Instant picnic hit!

In a zesty jicama salad.

Make the colorful citrus slaw on page 177, but use jicama matchsticks instead of the carrots and half the radishes. Brighten it all up with orange segments, jalapeño radish pickles, and fresh mint.

On a creamy avocado edamame dip.

Make a quick dip by pulsing avocado, edamame, garlic, and jalapeño radish pickle brine in a food processor until creamy. Serve with a pile of pickles on top!

For breakfast!

Stuff jalapeño radish pickles into a breakfast burrito or breakfast tacos with scrambled eggs, roasted potatoes, sliced avocado, and cilantro.

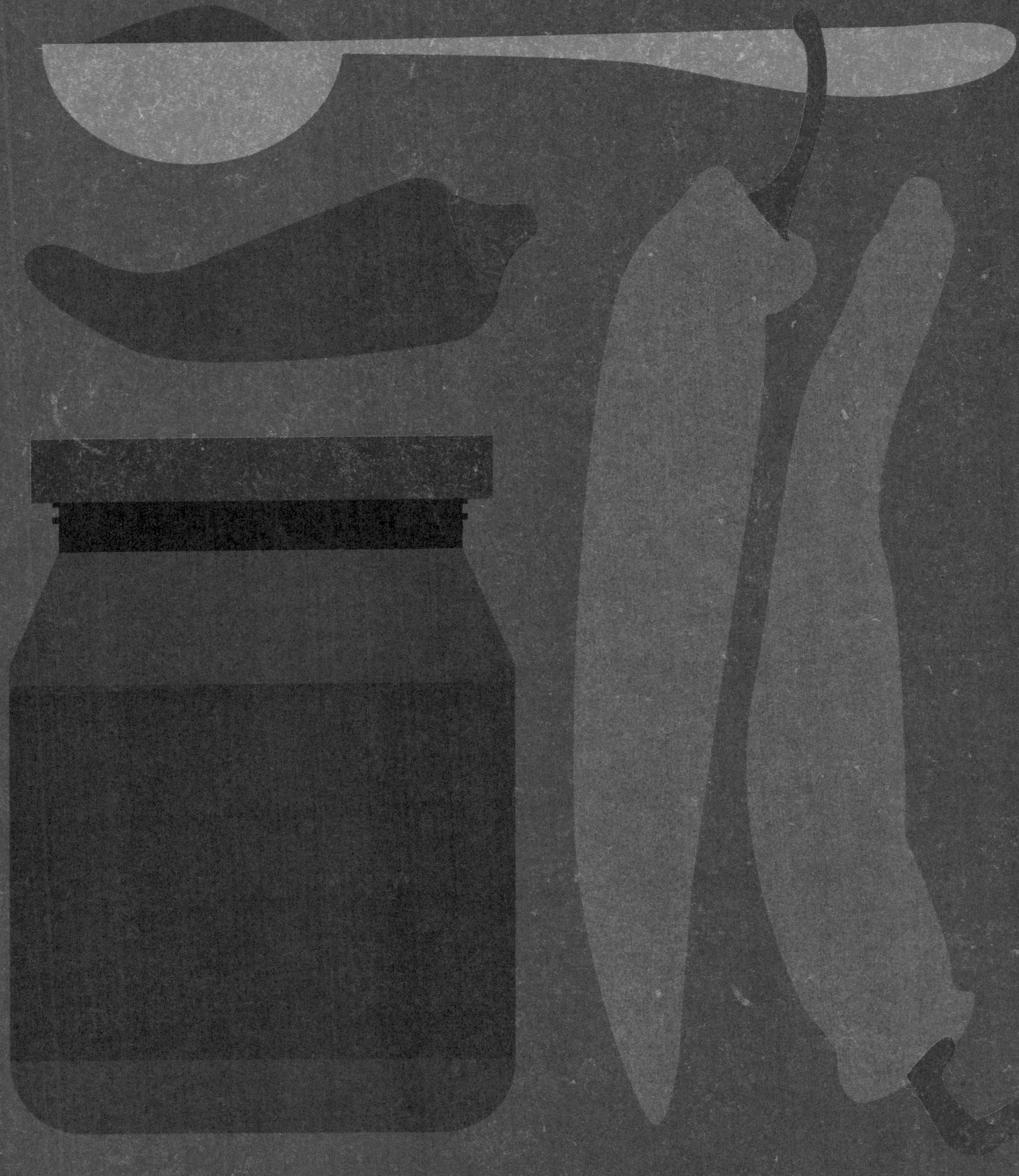

HARISSA

Despite what you might expect from a food person, I don't have a crazy amount of condiments in my fridge. I like to keep the exact amount of jars that fit in the door space—and not one more. That means I'm pretty selective. I keep only those I know I'll use over and over—the ones that can turn a boring meal into something exceptionally flavorful. Enter: harissa, a North African chile paste made with smoked or roasted peppers and aromatic spices like cumin and caraway. I always have it on hand, and I switch between two brands depending on who I'm having over for dinner that week. I like Mina harissa because it's easy to find at most grocery stores and mild in flavor (even their spicy version). I also like Trader Joe's, which is thicker and super spicy—great for spice lovers.

GOLDEN BEET SOUP

WITH LEMON HARISSA OIL

Don't let this simple beet soup fool you. Sure, it's humble, but that doesn't mean it's boring! I would even go so far as to say that it's one of my favorite recipes in this book. The soup itself is creamy and comforting, and a drizzle of the boldly spiced lemon harissa oil gives it an exciting pop of flavor. It's a perfect cozy meal for a cool fall or winter day.

2 tablespoons extra-virgin olive oil

1 medium yellow onion, chopped

2 garlic cloves, halved

½ teaspoon sea salt

Freshly ground black pepper

2 pounds golden beets (about 5), peeled and diced

1 tablespoon grated fresh ginger

4 cups vegetable broth

2 tablespoons fresh lemon juice

Whole milk Greek yogurt, for serving

Fresh cilantro leaves, for garnish

Aleppo pepper

Lemon Harissa Oil

⅓ cup extra-virgin olive oil

¼ teaspoon whole caraway seeds, crushed

¼ teaspoon whole coriander seeds, crushed

¼ teaspoon whole cumin seeds, crushed

1 teaspoon lemon zest

1 tablespoon spicy harissa

Heat the olive oil in a large pot or Dutch oven over medium heat. Add the onion, garlic, salt, and several grinds of pepper and cook, stirring occasionally, for 5 to 8 minutes, or until softened.

Add the beets and ginger and stir for 30 seconds. Add the broth and simmer, uncovered, for 25 to 45 minutes, or until the beets are tender. The broth should cover the beets throughout the cooking process. If it reduces too much, add water as needed to cover them.

Meanwhile, make the lemon harissa oil: Heat the olive oil in a small skillet over medium heat. Add the caraway, coriander, and cumin seeds and cook for 15 seconds to 1 minute, or until fragrant. Remove from the heat and transfer to a heatproof bowl. Stir in the lemon zest, followed by the harissa.

Allow the soup to cool slightly and transfer to a blender. Add the lemon juice and blend until smooth. Season to taste.

Ladle into bowls and top with a dollop of Greek yogurt and drizzles of the lemon harissa oil. Garnish with cilantro, sprinkle with Aleppo pepper, and serve.

SERVES **4** *TO* **6**

VEGAN: Skip the yogurt or use your favorite unsweetened vegan yogurt.

GLUTEN-FREE

TIP

Spice to your level! I've given you a wide range of how much harissa to add to the harissa mayo. Start with 2 tablespoons and add more to taste. The amount you like will depend on your individual heat tolerance and the brand of harissa you're using.

HARISSA-SPICED LENTIL BURGERS

WITH HARISSA MAYO

For as long as I've been creating recipes for Love & Lemons, I've been sneaking beets into dishes and lying to Jack about them. He doesn't like beets, but since I'm the one who cooks, I figure if he can't tell, no harm, no foul. I added just a little grated beet to these patties for a hint of sweetness to balance the spicy harissa. It was supposed to be my secret, but to my surprise, they turned out bright pink! Jack looked at them suspiciously . . . and then ate two. The caraway seeds and harissa give these burgers a delicious earthy, spicy flavor, but it's the creamy harissa mayo that really takes them over the top.

3 cups cooked green lentils, drained and rinsed (page 321)

½ cup grated red beet, grated on the large holes of a box grater

⅓ cup grated yellow onion, grated on the large holes of a box grater

⅓ cup spicy harissa

2 tablespoons apple cider vinegar

3 garlic cloves, grated

¾ teaspoon sea salt

½ teaspoon ground cumin

½ teaspoon whole caraway seeds, crushed

1 large egg

1½ cups panko bread crumbs

Extra-virgin olive oil, for brushing

6 hamburger buns, for serving

Sauerkraut, for serving

Arugula, lettuce, radicchio, and/or sunflower sprouts, for serving

Harissa Mayo

1 cup mayonnaise

2 to 8 tablespoons spicy harissa

In a large bowl, combine the lentils, beet, onion, harissa, apple cider vinegar, garlic, salt, cumin, and caraway seeds. Use a potato masher or fork to mash until the mixture holds together but still has some visible lentil pieces. Add the egg and use a spatula to fold until combined. Fold in the panko.

Use your hands to form the mixture into six 1-inch-thick patties, a heaping ½ cup each. The mixture should be cohesive and a little wet. If it's too wet to handle, chill it in the refrigerator for 20 minutes to firm up or mash the lentils a little more.

Heat a cast-iron skillet over medium heat and brush with olive oil. Working in batches if necessary, cook the burgers for 5 to 8 minutes per side, or until charred on both sides and cooked through. Reduce the heat as needed if the burgers are browning too quickly.

Make the harissa mayo: In a small bowl, stir together the mayonnaise and 2 tablespoons harissa, adding more harissa as needed to reach your desired spice level.

Assemble the burgers on the buns with a slather of the harissa mayo, sauerkraut, and arugula.

SERVES **6**

GLUTEN-FREE: Use gluten-free panko and gluten-free buns.

STAUB
STAUB
mina

ONE-POT CHICKPEA SWEET POTATO STEW

WITH HARISSA

This is a recipe where the oven does the work for you. It's a spiced-up riff on a dish I love from Yotam Ottolenghi and Noor Murad's mouthwatering cookbook *Shelf Love*. The beauty of it is that everything goes into one pot—harissa paste, chickpeas, sweet potatoes, tomatoes, olive oil, and crushed spices—and it cooks, covered, for about an hour. With the exception of a few stirs, you can walk away, play with your kids, maybe read Love & Lemons on your phone while enjoying the aromatic smells wafting out of the oven. The end result is a flavorful stew that's so much more than the sum of its parts. Serve it with a simple lemon yogurt sauce for bright contrast.

3 cups cooked chickpeas, drained and rinsed (page 320)

1 medium sweet potato, chopped into 1-inch pieces

1 pint cherry tomatoes

¼ cup spicy harissa

4 garlic cloves, grated

1 tablespoon grated fresh ginger

2 teaspoons whole coriander seeds, crushed

2 teaspoons whole cumin seeds, crushed

1 teaspoon sea salt

½ teaspoon ground turmeric

Pinch of Aleppo pepper

¾ cup water

½ cup extra-virgin olive oil

Chopped fresh cilantro, for garnish

Lemon Yogurt

½ cup whole milk Greek yogurt

2 teaspoons fresh lemon juice

¼ teaspoon sea salt

Preheat the oven to 400°F.

In a medium Dutch oven, place the chickpeas, sweet potato, cherry tomatoes, harissa, garlic, ginger, coriander seeds, cumin seeds, salt, turmeric, and Aleppo pepper. Add the water and olive oil and stir until well combined.

Cover and bake for 30 minutes, then remove from the oven and stir. Cover and bake for another 25 to 30 minutes, or until the sweet potatoes are very tender and falling apart and the stew is thick. Remove from the oven and season to taste.

Meanwhile, make the lemon yogurt: In a small bowl, stir together the yogurt, lemon juice, and salt. The yogurt should have a creamy, dollopable consistency. If it's too thick, add water, 1 teaspoon at a time, as needed to loosen it.

Ladle the stew into bowls and serve topped with dollops of the lemon yogurt and cilantro.

SERVES **4**

VEGAN: Replace the Greek yogurt with ¾ cup blended silken tofu.

GLUTEN-FREE

MORE WAYS TO USE

HARISSA

On roasted veggies.

Toss cauliflower, sweet potatoes, or winter squash with harissa before roasting.

As a potato upgrade.

Serve roasted potatoes, smashed potatoes, or French fries with the harissa mayo on page 103.

To spice up classic sauces.

Mix a little harissa into BBQ sauce to give it an unexpected kick (great for dipping!). I also fell in love with adding harissa to marinara when I was testing the Summer Lasagna on pages 158–59 of my last book, *Simple Feel Good Food*. Such an easy way to kick a simple pasta up a notch!

On elote, with a twist.

Brush grilled corn on the cob with harissa mayo (page 103). Sprinkle with crumbled feta and chopped parsley!

In vegetarian chili.

For a fun spin on your favorite chili recipe, replace the chili powder with harissa.

In tasty weeknight tacos.

Fill tortillas with a dollop of crema (page 321), black beans, and harissa-roasted sweet potatoes. Top with vinegar slaw (page 171) for crunch!

In a mouthwatering yogurt sauce.

Mix harissa into whole milk Greek yogurt to make a creamy, spicy, aromatic sauce you'll want to put on everything. I love to serve a swoosh of it under grilled or roasted vegetable dishes. One of my favorite combinations is harissa yogurt + grilled eggplant + toasted walnuts + feta + mint.

GIARDINIERA

When I moved back to Chicago, I started keeping a jar of giardiniera on hand at all times. I put it on pizza or pasta . . . I'd even stir it into scrambled eggs or spoon it over my morning avocado toast to start the day with some punch. I was in my giardiniera era. If you're not familiar, giardiniera is a spicy, tangy, oily vegetable condiment typically served with Italian beef sandwiches. I wanted to include a homemade version in this book because we realized the good stuff (aka Chicago-style) isn't necessarily sold nationwide. We also wanted ours to be a little fresher—and a lot more colorful. Note: At first, the salt-brined veggies might taste overly salty, but trust the process—after chilling overnight in oil and vinegar, the flavors balance out.

TIP

The following recipes are best with our homemade giardiniera. For a store-bought option, we like That Pickle Guy's spicy giardiniera, available in the Chicagoland area or online. If you're looking for another brand, be sure it's Chicago-style rather than Italian-style, and check the label to confirm it was made in Chicago. Some common grocery store brands we tested were too chunky, too salty, or lacked the right tang.

1 cup very small cauliflower florets

½ red bell pepper, stemmed, seeded, and diced

2 celery ribs, diced

1 medium carrot, diced

2 jalapeño peppers, stemmed and diced

3 serrano peppers, stemmed and diced

6 pepperoncini, stemmed and diced

⅓ cup mixed olives, pitted and diced

2 tablespoons sea salt

1 cup distilled white vinegar

½ cup extra-virgin olive oil

1 garlic clove, thinly sliced

1 teaspoon dried oregano

1 teaspoon red pepper flakes

½ teaspoon whole celery seeds

In a medium bowl, stir together the cauliflower, red bell pepper, celery, carrot, jalapeños, serranos, pepperoncini, and olives. Add the salt and stir until dissolved. Cover and chill in the refrigerator for 6 hours or overnight.

Transfer the vegetables to a fine-mesh strainer and rinse under cool running water to remove the excess salt.

In a 28-ounce or similar-size lidded jar, stir together the vinegar, olive oil, garlic, oregano, red pepper flakes, and celery seeds. Add the rinsed vegetables and stir, pushing down to submerge them in the brine. Cover and chill in the refrigerator overnight before using.

Store in the refrigerator for up to 2 weeks.

YIELD: ABOUT **3** *CUPS*

VEGAN | GLUTEN-FREE

PULLED MUSHROOM SANDWICHES

WITH GIARDINIERA

When I was growing up in Chicago, Italian beef sandwiches (which are now iconic, thanks to *The Bear*) were a regular occurrence at my family gatherings. I still crave them every so often, but since beef isn't my thing anymore, I make this fun mushroom version instead! I pull king oyster mushrooms apart with a fork to create a sliced meat texture. Then, I sauté them with a bold spice mix and broth to create plenty of "au jus" for a drippy sandwich. Top it with onions, peppers, and lots of tangy, spicy giardiniera. Napkins for serving, not optional!

12 ounces king oyster mushrooms

2 tablespoons extra-virgin olive oil

1 red bell pepper, stemmed, seeded, and sliced

½ medium yellow onion, thinly sliced

¼ teaspoon sea salt

Freshly ground black pepper

1 teaspoon dried oregano

1 teaspoon garlic powder

1 teaspoon ground coriander

1 teaspoon whole fennel seeds, crushed

½ teaspoon smoked paprika

1 tablespoon tamari

¾ cup vegetable broth

4 (5-inch) French rolls or soft baguette pieces, warmed

Giardiniera (page 108), for serving

Slice off the tops of the mushrooms and cut them into thin strips. Drag the tines of a fork down the mushroom stems to start to shred them, then use your hands to pull them apart into long strips.

Heat 1½ teaspoons of the olive oil in a large skillet over medium-high heat. Add the red bell pepper, onion, salt, and several grinds of pepper. Cook, stirring occasionally, for 10 to 12 minutes, or until tender and browned in places. Remove from the pan and set aside.

Wipe out the pan and return to medium-high heat. Add the remaining 1½ tablespoons olive oil and the mushrooms. Cook, stirring occasionally, for 1 to 2 minutes, or until the mushrooms are browned. Add the oregano, garlic powder, coriander, fennel seeds, smoked paprika, and several grinds of pepper and cook, stirring, for 2 more minutes, or until the spices are fragrant.

Add the tamari and vegetable broth and stir, scraping up any browned bits on the bottom of the pan. Reduce the heat to medium-low and cook for 2 to 4 minutes, or until the broth has reduced slightly.

Assemble sandwiches in the rolls with the mushrooms, peppers and onions, and scoops of giardiniera. Serve immediately.

SERVES **4**

VEGAN

GLUTEN-FREE: Use certified gluten-free tamari and gluten-free bread.

TIP

Spice to your level! Pile on more giardiniera for a hotter dip, or use less for a milder flavor. When I serve this dip to my family, I divide it into two separate bowls: one with less giardiniera for my mom and sister, and one with (a lot) more for my brother-in-law Josh and me.

SPICY SPINACH PARTY DIP

WITH GIARDINIERA

After we made our homemade giardiniera, we had fun coming up with different ways to use it. The "beef sandwich" was an obvious choice, which got us thinking about other Midwestern favorites . . . which led us to making this colorful twist on a classic spinach party dip. I'll say it—I like it even more than the original! It's made with a tangy Greek yogurt base (instead of sour cream and cream cheese), fresh spinach, and spicy giardiniera. For extra kick and color, more giardiniera is sprinkled like confetti on top.

5 ounces fresh spinach

1½ cups thick whole milk Greek yogurt (we like Fage or Chobani)

½ teaspoon onion powder

½ teaspoon sea salt*

½ cup Giardiniera (page 108), drained, plus more as needed

Toasted baguette slices, for serving

**Store-bought giardiniera can be salty! If you're using it here, omit the ½ teaspoon salt in the dip. Season to taste before serving.*

Place the spinach in a steamer basket and set over a pot filled with 1 inch of water. Bring the water to a simmer, cover, and steam for 1 minute, or until the spinach is wilted. Transfer to a strainer and squeeze out the excess water. Roughly chop the spinach and set aside to cool slightly.

In a medium bowl, stir together the yogurt, onion powder, salt, and half of the giardiniera. Add the spinach and stir to combine. Chill in the refrigerator for at least 30 minutes and up to 1 day to allow the flavors to develop.

When ready to serve, stir, then transfer the dip to a serving dish and top with the remaining giardiniera, adding more as needed to lightly cover the top. Serve with toasted baguette slices.

SERVES **8**

VEGAN: Replace the Greek yogurt with whipped tofu (page 322).

GLUTEN-FREE: Serve with gluten-free crackers or baguette.

SHEET PAN PIZZA CAULIFLOWER

WITH GIARDINIERA

Okay, this isn't pizza, I get it. So what is it? It's pizza cauliflower! I take everything I like *on* my pizza—arugula, radicchio, red onion, and lots of spicy giardiniera—and top it onto cauliflower that's been roasted with pizza-y spices and melty cheese. Think of it as a fork-and-knife salad that's totally satisfying and packed with pizza flavor! Tip: When you add the cheese, don't worry if some of it falls in between the cauliflower pieces. It'll get nicely browned and bubbly as it bakes and help hold everything together.

1 medium cauliflower (about 2 pounds)

2 tablespoons extra-virgin olive oil

1 teaspoon garlic powder

½ teaspoon dried oregano

½ teaspoon sea salt

½ teaspoon whole fennel seeds, crushed

Freshly ground black pepper

6 ounces fresh mozzarella cheese, torn into pieces

1 cup grated provolone cheese

1½ cups arugula

1½ cups thinly sliced radicchio

½ cup thinly sliced red onion

½ cup Giardiniera (page 108), drained, plus more for serving

Red pepper flakes

Shaved Parmesan cheese, for garnish

Preheat the oven to 450°F and line a large baking sheet with parchment paper.

Remove any tough outer leaves from the cauliflower, then slice the cauliflower into 1-inch-thick slabs. Slices from the center will stay intact and form "steaks," while outer slices will fall apart into florets. Cut the steaks in half through the core to form two slabs and cut any large florets into roughly 1½-inch pieces.

Arrange the cauliflower slabs evenly on the baking sheet. Fill in the gaps between them with the florets. Drizzle with the olive oil. Sprinkle with the garlic powder, oregano, salt, fennel seeds, and several grinds of pepper and use your hands to coat. Roast for 25 to 30 minutes, or until tender and browned around the edges.

Remove the cauliflower from the oven and arrange the mozzarella and provolone evenly on top. Bake for 5 minutes, or until the cheese is melted, then turn on the broiler and broil for 2 to 5 minutes, or until the cheese is browned and bubbling.

In a large bowl, toss together the arugula, radicchio, red onion, and half the giardiniera. Sprinkle over the cauliflower and top with the remaining giardiniera, red pepper flakes, and shaved Parmesan. Serve with more giardiniera on the side.

SERVES **4**

GLUTEN-FREE

MORE WAYS TO USE

GIARDINIERA

On an antipasto platter.

Pair it with your favorite cheeses, crackers or crostini, and fresh veggies.

In a bagel schmear.

Our favorite Chicago bakery, Mindy's, makes the BEST bagels with giardiniera cream cheese. I love it so much that I've started making my own at home—just mix drained giardiniera with cream cheese or vegan cream cheese for a flavor-packed bagel topping.

In an Italian chopped salad

with iceberg lettuce, radicchio, artichoke hearts, cherry tomatoes, chickpeas, and big shavings of Parm. Bonus: The oily giardiniera brine will add an extra punch to the dressing!

On an epic Italian party sub

with lemony smashed white beans, sliced provolone cheese, tomatoes, crisp iceberg lettuce, and red onion.

On pizza.

A must for me when my family is ordering delivery in Chicago. Try it with mushrooms, red onion, and spinach. You'll be hooked!

In a picnic-perfect potato salad.

If you ask me, the brighter and brinier a potato salad is, the better. Make a great one with scallions, fresh chives and dill, and a big scoop of giardiniera. Dress it with a splash of giardiniera brine, olive oil, mustard, and a little mayo.

SPICY TURMERIC PASTE

If there's one spicy condiment you should make all the time, it's this one! It's the simplest of them all—just stir the ingredients together, and in 5 minutes or less, you'll have the tastiest flavor booster ready to elevate so many dishes. With a concentrated amount of miso, ginger, and curry spices, it works as a flavorful marinade, a punchy soup base, and a delicious sauce starter.

- ⅓ cup avocado oil
- ⅓ cup fresh lemon juice
- ⅓ cup white miso paste
- 1 tablespoon grated fresh ginger
- 2 teaspoons curry powder
- 2 teaspoons ground turmeric
- 1½ teaspoons cayenne pepper

YIELD: ABOUT **1** *CUP*

VEGAN | GLUTEN-FREE

In a medium bowl, whisk together the avocado oil, lemon juice, miso paste, ginger, curry powder, turmeric, and cayenne.

Store in an airtight container in the refrigerator for up to 1 week. This paste also freezes well for up to 3 months. I like to freeze it in ice cube trays so that I can use a little at a time.

TIP For a milder turmeric paste, reduce or skip the cayenne.

TURMERIC TOFU BANH MI

WITH SPICY TURMERIC PASTE

This recipe is a vegetarian spin on a banh mi, a Vietnamese sandwich filled with pickled vegetables, cilantro, mayo, and typically meat such as grilled pork. This version is inspired by a sandwich from Farmhouse Deli, a café halfway between Chicago and our cottage in Northern Michigan. Their turmeric tofu banh mi is so delicious that it makes our five-hour drive entirely worth it. I don't just crave this sandwich: I dream about it, so I had to create a version I could easily make at home. The spicy turmeric paste makes this recipe a breeze. Slather some on the tofu before baking, and mix a little more into mayo for a tasty spiced sandwich spread.

Marinated Veggies

1 small carrot, peeled into ribbons

¼ English cucumber, halved lengthwise and peeled into ribbons

½ watermelon radish or 2 red radishes, sliced into thin rounds or half-moons

1 jalapeño pepper, stemmed and very thinly sliced on the bias

2 tablespoons rice vinegar

¼ teaspoon cane sugar

¼ teaspoon sea salt

For the Sandwiches

1 (16-ounce) block high-protein tofu, patted dry and cut crosswise into 8 slabs

¼ cup plus 2 teaspoons Spicy Turmeric Paste (page 118)

½ cup mayonnaise

4 (5-inch) baguette pieces

Fresh cilantro leaves

Sriracha, for serving

Preheat the oven to 425°F and line a baking sheet with parchment paper.

Make the marinated veggies: In a large bowl, toss the carrots, cucumbers, radishes, and jalapeños with the rice vinegar, sugar, and salt. Chill in the refrigerator until ready to serve.

Make the sandwiches: Arrange the tofu slabs evenly on the baking sheet and brush with ¼ cup of the spicy turmeric paste, flipping to coat all sides. Bake for 20 minutes, or until browned around the edges.

In a small bowl, mix the remaining 2 teaspoons spicy turmeric paste with the mayonnaise.

Slice the baguette pieces in half lengthwise and slather both cut sides with the turmeric mayonnaise. Fill each sandwich with two of the tofu slabs, the marinated veggies, and cilantro. Serve with sriracha.

SERVES **4**

VEGAN: Use vegan mayonnaise.

GLUTEN-FREE: Use gluten-free bread.

INSTANT CURRY NOODLE SOUP

WITH SPICY TURMERIC PASTE

The ultimate make-ahead lunch! These flavors are everything I crave in a Thai noodle soup but simplified for easy weekday prep. The spicy turmeric paste is SUCH a delicious flavor booster—just place a dab into each jar and load in the veggies and noodles. When you're ready to eat, add the coconut milk mixture, heat, and shake. We like to finish each jar with a big squeeze of lime juice for extra brightness.

¼ cup Spicy Turmeric Paste (page 118)

8 ounces rice vermicelli noodles (we like Lotus Foods pho rice noodles)

2 cups fresh spinach

½ red bell pepper, stemmed, seeded, and very thinly sliced

1 medium or 2 small carrots, cut into thin matchsticks

2 scallions, thinly sliced

2 (13.5-ounce) cans full-fat coconut milk

1½ cups water

Lime wedges, for serving

Sea salt

Place 1 tablespoon of the spicy turmeric paste at the bottom of four 16-ounce or similar-size microwave-safe lidded jars. Divide the uncooked noodles among the jars, breaking them if necessary to fit. Divide the spinach, red pepper, carrots, and scallions among the jars. It might be a tight squeeze. That's okay! Cover and chill in the refrigerator for up to 5 days until ready to make the soup.

Combine the coconut milk and water in a large microwave-safe bowl or liquid measuring cup. Stir until well combined. If your coconut milk has solids that are difficult to break down, microwave in 30-second bursts until smooth. Evenly divide the mixture among four airtight containers or jars, adding about 1¼ cups liquid to each. Cover and chill in the refrigerator for up to 5 days until ready to make the soup.

To make one serving of the soup, pour one jar of the coconut milk mixture into one of the jars of noodles. Microwave uncovered for 2 to 4 minutes, or until boiling, checking every minute so that the jar doesn't bubble over. Cover and shake (careful—the sides of the jar will be hot!). Let stand for 3 to 7 minutes, or until the noodles are tender, shaking every few minutes to make sure the noodles are submerged in the liquid.

If the noodles aren't fully cooked after 7 minutes, microwave uncovered for an additional 30 seconds, or longer as needed, to soften them. The exact timing will depend on the brand of noodles you're using. Stir, then squeeze a lime wedge into the jar. Season to taste with salt and enjoy.

SERVES **4** | **VEGAN** | **GLUTEN-FREE:** Use gluten-free rice noodles.

PANEER & PEPPER RICE BOWL

WITH SPICY TURMERIC PASTE

This is a new version of a recipe that got cut from our previous book, *Simple Feel Good Food*, at the last minute. The original recipe featured grilled paneer skewers in a curry yogurt marinade, and while we adored the flavor combination, we had trouble with them sticking to the grill. We don't ever want a recipe to be fussy to make, so we thought, if you can't fix it—sheet pan it! To make things even easier, our spicy turmeric paste mixed with yogurt works as both a coating for the baked paneer and a flavorful sauce for the bowls.

1 cup whole milk Greek yogurt

2 tablespoons Spicy Turmeric Paste (page 118)

¼ teaspoon sea salt, plus more for sprinkling

8 ounces paneer cheese, cut into 1-inch cubes

4 jalapeño peppers, stemmed and roughly chopped

2 red bell peppers, stemmed, seeded, and cut into 1-inch pieces

1 small red onion, cut into thin wedges

Avocado oil, for drizzling

2 cups cooked brown rice (page 320)

¼ cup fresh cilantro leaves

¼ cup fresh mint leaves

Preheat the oven to 425°F and line two large baking sheets with parchment paper.

In a medium bowl, mix together the yogurt, spicy turmeric paste, and salt. The sauce should have a creamy, dollopable consistency. If it's too thick, add water, 1 tablespoon at a time, as needed to loosen it.

Place the paneer in the center of one of the baking sheets. Top with ⅓ cup of the turmeric yogurt sauce and toss to coat. Spread evenly on the baking sheet. Chill the remaining yogurt sauce in the refrigerator until ready to serve.

Place the jalapeños and red bell peppers on one side of the second baking sheet and the onion wedges on the other side. Drizzle with avocado oil, sprinkle with salt, and toss to coat. Spread evenly on the baking sheet.

Place both baking sheets in the oven. Roast the paneer for 15 to 20 minutes, or until well browned underneath. Roast the vegetables for 20 to 25 minutes, or until tender and browned around the edges.

Assemble bowls with the rice, paneer, and roasted vegetables. Top each serving with a dollop of the reserved turmeric yogurt sauce, the cilantro, and mint. Season to taste and serve with the remaining sauce on the side.

SERVES **4**

GLUTEN-FREE

MORE WAYS TO USE

SPICY TURMERIC PASTE

On roasted cauliflower.

Toss to coat the florets in the paste before roasting.

In a creamy golden dressing.

Mix the paste with a little coconut milk to make a super-easy, delicious dressing. Try it on the Crunchy Snap Pea and Napa Cabbage Salad on page 155 or on hearty lunch salad with kale, roasted carrots, roasted chickpeas, and pepitas.

In a next-level pot of rice.

Stir a little paste into freshly cooked rice to give it a bold yellow color and bright, spicy flavor.

In a quick couscous pilaf.

For a 15-minute side dish, toss the paste with freshly cooked couscous, grated carrots, golden raisins, parsley, and toasted almonds.

In the one-pot chickpea stew

on page 105. No harissa handy? Use spicy turmeric paste instead.

In a cozy butternut squash soup.

Sauté a sliced onion until softened, then add grated garlic and ginger, chopped butternut squash, and coconut milk and simmer until tender. Stir in some spicy turmeric paste for a quick flavor boost, then blend until smooth.

In a fun yellow noodle bowl.

Add some of the paste to cooked noodles while they're still warm, tossing until they're coated in a yellow sauce. Serve topped with baked tofu (page 321 or store-bought), cucumbers, and blanched snap peas. You could even throw on some Coconut Curry Peanuts (page 150)!

In a red lentil soup or dal.

It's a super-easy way to add depth at the end of the cooking process.

CHAPTER 3

LEMON ZA'ATAR BREAD CRUMBS
SESAME NORI CRISP
COCONUT CURRY PEANUTS
SPICED ALMOND CRUNCH
MIX & MATCH CRUNCHY VEGGIE SLAWS

CRUNCHY

What do potato chips, popcorn, and pretzels have in common? Crunch! But this craveable quality shouldn't just belong to snacks—in this chapter, I create exciting textural *meals* using seedy sprinkles, crispy toppings, toasty nuts, and vibrant veg slaws. That's right—vegetables can be crunchy too!

LEMON ZA'ATAR BREAD CRUMBS

We couldn't have a crunchy chapter without toasty bread crumbs—they're the ultimate ingredient to have on hand for quickly adding texture to so many dishes! But these aren't just any bread crumbs—they have lemon zest for brightness and za'atar for a tangy, herbal note. Za'atar is available at most grocery stores these days, but if you can't find it locally, you can order it online—I especially like the Burlap & Barrel brand.

8 ounces stale sourdough bread, roughly torn (about 4 cups)

2 tablespoons extra-virgin olive oil

½ teaspoon sea salt

2 teaspoons lemon zest

2 teaspoons za'atar

YIELD: ABOUT **2½** *CUPS*

VEGAN

Preheat the oven to 350°F and line a baking sheet with parchment paper.

Place the bread in a food processor. For coarse bread crumbs, pulse until some of the bread is finely ground but some coarser pieces remain. For fine bread crumbs, pulse until all the bread is finely ground.

Transfer the bread crumbs to the baking sheet. Drizzle with the olive oil, sprinkle with the salt, and toss to coat. Spread evenly on the baking sheet and bake for 15 to 25 minutes, or until crisp and deeply golden brown.

While the bread crumbs are still warm, transfer to a large bowl and toss with the lemon zest and za'atar. Allow to cool to room temperature.

Store in an airtight container at room temperature for up to 4 days.

FENNEL PARMESAN

WITH LEMON ZA'ATAR BREAD CRUMBS

If you love eggplant Parmesan and you love fennel, you'll love this fennel Parmesan! And if you're on the fence about fennel, be prepared to become friends, because everyone we've served this to—even Ollie, my four-year-old—goes back for seconds. Planks of fennel are roasted until tender, then layered with cheese and tomato sauce and baked with lots of crispy lemon za'atar bread crumbs on top.

4 medium fennel bulbs (about 3 pounds with fronds, 2¼ pounds without)

Extra-virgin olive oil, for drizzling

Sea salt and freshly ground black pepper

3 cups marinara sauce (we like Rao's)

8 ounces fresh mozzarella cheese, torn into pieces

⅔ cup freshly grated Parmesan cheese

Heaping 1 cup coarse Lemon Za'atar Bread Crumbs (page 130)

Red pepper flakes

Fresh basil leaves, for garnish

Preheat the oven to 425°F and line two large baking sheets with parchment paper. Brush an 8×11-inch or similar baking dish with olive oil.

If the fennel bulbs have fronds, trim them off and save them for another use. Quarter the fennel bulbs lengthwise and cut out and discard the tough cores. Slice each quarter lengthwise into ¼-inch-thick planks.

Spread the fennel planks evenly on the baking sheets. Drizzle with olive oil and sprinkle with salt and pepper. Rub lightly with your hands to coat. Cover the baking sheets with foil and roast for 20 minutes, or until the fennel is fork-tender. Uncover and roast for another 20 minutes, or until the fennel is browned.

Spread 2 cups of the marinara sauce at the bottom of the prepared baking dish.

Arrange half the fennel evenly over the sauce. Top with half the mozzarella and half the Parmesan. Layer on the remaining fennel followed by the remaining 1 cup marinara sauce, the remaining mozzarella, and remaining Parmesan. Sprinkle the bread crumbs evenly on top.

Bake uncovered for 20 to 25 minutes, or until the cheese is melted and beginning to brown.

Remove from the oven and let stand for 10 minutes. Sprinkle with red pepper flakes, garnish with basil, and serve.

SERVES **6**

CRISPY CHICKPEA FRITTERS

WITH LEMON ZA'ATAR BREAD CRUMBS

You'll use the lemon za'atar bread crumbs in two ways in this recipe: Some go into the fritter mixture to help bind it together. More coat the outsides of the fritters, giving them a delicious crispy crust. Serve them with a zesty fennel slaw to up the crunch factor even more, plus a dollop of crema for a little creamy contrast. Leftover fritters—if you have any—freeze well.

Fennel Slaw

4 cups thinly sliced fennel (about 2 medium bulbs)

1 cup thinly sliced red onion

3 tablespoons fresh lemon juice

1 tablespoon extra-virgin olive oil

½ teaspoon sea salt

For the Fritters

2 cups cooked chickpeas, drained and rinsed (page 320)

2 large eggs, lightly beaten

⅔ cup chopped scallions

½ cup chopped fresh cilantro

3 tablespoons fresh lemon juice, plus wedges for serving

3 tablespoons tahini

3 garlic cloves, grated

¾ teaspoon sea salt

Freshly ground black pepper

1¾ cups fine Lemon Za'atar Bread Crumbs (page 130)

Extra-virgin olive oil, for the pan

Crema (page 321), for serving

Aleppo pepper (optional)

Make the fennel slaw: In a large bowl, toss together the fennel, red onion, lemon juice, olive oil, and salt. Season to taste and chill in the refrigerator until ready to serve.

Make the fritters: Place the chickpeas in another large bowl. Use a potato masher to mash them until they are mostly broken down but a few larger pieces remain intact. Add the eggs, scallions, cilantro, lemon juice, tahini, garlic, salt, and several grinds of pepper and mix until well combined. Fold in 1 cup of the bread crumbs.

Place the remaining ¾ cup bread crumbs in a shallow dish. Use your hands to form the chickpea mixture into eight ½-inch-thick patties, roughly ⅓ cup each. Coat in the bread crumbs.

Heat a cast-iron skillet over medium heat and coat the bottom with olive oil. Working in batches if necessary, add the chickpea fritters and cook for 3 to 4 minutes per side, or until golden brown and cooked through, reducing the heat as needed if the fritters are browning too quickly. If working in batches, wipe out the pan and add more oil after each one.

Serve topped with crema, the fennel slaw, and Aleppo pepper, if desired.

SERVES **4**

ONE-PAN BEANS & GREENS

WITH LEMON ZA'ATAR BREAD CRUMBS

If you start making this recipe and halfway through you think, "Hmm . . . this seems a little boring. There are beans, more beans, greens . . . Healthy—yes. But exciting?!" Okay, that's what I thought too when I made this the first time. And then those game-changing bread crumbs went on and elevated the whole dish. It's been one of my weeknight favorites ever since.

¼ cup extra-virgin olive oil

½ medium yellow onion, chopped

1 bunch Swiss chard, stems chopped, leaves torn

¾ teaspoon sea salt

Freshly ground black pepper

3 cups cooked navy beans, drained and rinsed (page 320)

¾ cup water

3 garlic cloves, grated

1 teaspoon Dijon mustard

3 tablespoons fresh lemon juice

1 cup coarse Lemon Za'atar Bread Crumbs (page 130)

½ teaspoon red pepper flakes

¼ cup chopped fresh parsley

Heat 3 tablespoons of the olive oil in a large skillet over medium heat. Add the onion, chard stems, salt, and several grinds of pepper and cook, stirring occasionally, for 3 to 5 minutes, or until softened.

Reduce the heat to medium-low and add the beans, water, garlic, and mustard and stir. Add the chard leaves. Depending on the size of your pan, they may not all fit at once. If necessary, add some and let them wilt slightly before adding the rest. Cook, stirring occasionally, for 2 to 4 minutes, or until the chard is wilted but still bright green.

Remove from the heat, stir in the lemon juice, and season to taste.

Spread the beans evenly in the skillet. Drizzle with the remaining 1 tablespoon olive oil and sprinkle with the bread crumbs and red pepper flakes. Garnish with the parsley and serve.

SERVES **4**

VEGAN

MORE WAYS TO USE

LEMON ZA'ATAR BREAD CRUMBS

On just about any pasta.

Sprinkle the bread crumbs on right before serving—they'll add a delightful, delicate crunch!

In Mediterranean stuffed mushrooms

with grated pecorino, sun-dried tomatoes, pine nuts, and parsley.

On a bright and briny radicchio salad.

Who needs croutons when you have lemon za'atar bread crumbs?! Shower them over a salad made with chopped radicchio, chickpeas, shaved fennel, thinly sliced red onion, olives, pepperoncini, parsley, and basil. Toss with your favorite Italian dressing or the lemon vinaigrette on page 282. Or skip the herbs and toss with the Italian salsa verde on page 67!

On crispy cauliflower.

Use fine lemon za'atar bread crumbs to bread cauliflower florets or slabs for a crave-worthy sandwich filling, side dish, or snack! Follow the method from the Crispy Cauliflower Sandwiches on page 245, using the lemon za'atar bread crumbs instead of the panko and omitting the smoked paprika.

On baked mac and cheese.

Crispy bread crumbs + creamy pasta = total deliciousness.

Over baked feta.

Place a block of feta in a small baking dish and nestle cherry tomatoes around it. Drizzle with olive oil and broil until the cheese is browned and the tomatoes are bursty, then top with the bread crumbs and fresh basil. Serve with crostini for scooping it all up.

SESAME NORI CRISP

& BONUS SHALLOT OIL

Ever since we started traveling to Japan, one of my favorite condiments has been furikake—a toasted nori and sesame mixture that's on the table wherever rice is served—which is nearly everywhere. This recipe is my homemade take. Nori adds that unmistakable umami flavor, and fried shallots make it wonderfully crispy. It takes a little time to prepare, but I promise it's totally worth it. It's not only great with the three recipes in this chapter, but I also love it daily on scrambled eggs, noodles, and many other dishes. (See page 148 for more ways to use it!) And as a bonus, once you make the nori crisp, you'll have shallot-infused oil left over. Two condiments for the price of one!

5 ounces shallots (about 3 large or 6 small), cut into thin rings

1½ cups vegetable oil

½ cup black and white sesame seeds

½ cup panko bread crumbs

1½ sheets nori, cut into 1-inch pieces

½ teaspoon sea salt

Set a fine-mesh strainer over a heatproof bowl. Preheat the oven to 350°F and line a baking sheet with parchment paper.

In a medium saucepan, combine the shallots and vegetable oil. Cook over medium-low heat for 15 to 30 minutes, or until the shallots are a deep amber color. The oil will start to boil in the first few minutes of cooking and should continue bubbling for the remainder of the cooking process. Watch the shallots closely after about 12 minutes of cooking. As soon as some start to turn brown, the rest will darken fairly quickly. Reduce the heat to low as needed to prevent them from burning. When the shallots are dark amber, quickly remove the pan from the heat and pour the shallots and oil into the strainer set over the bowl.

Spread the shallots on a paper towel–lined plate and set them aside for 5 minutes to crisp up. Transfer the shallot oil to a jar or an airtight container.

Spread the sesame seeds on one half of the prepared baking sheet and the panko on the other half. Toss the panko with 2 teaspoons of the shallot oil and spread in an even layer. Bake for 10 minutes, or until the panko is golden brown.

Place the nori and shallots in a food processor and briefly pulse to break down the nori. Add the sesame seeds, panko, and salt and pulse until well combined.

Store the sesame nori crisp in an airtight container at room temperature for up to 3 days or in the freezer for up to 2 months. Store the shallot oil in an airtight container or jar at room temperature for up to 2 weeks.

YIELD: ABOUT **1 3/4** *CUPS*

VEGAN | **GLUTEN-FREE:** Use gluten-free panko.

STAUB

CARAMELIZED ONION PASTA

WITH SESAME NORI CRISP

When I first started making our sesame nori crisp, I was so happy to discover that it froze well. I didn't have to worry about polishing off a whole batch in a few days—instead, I could keep this savory sprinkle on hand at all times! With it ready to go, this oniony pasta is the simplest pantry meal. We cheat the caramelized onion process a bit here. Rather than cooking the onions low and slow for an hour, we cook them over medium heat for 20 minutes, then splash in a little tamari and balsamic to bring out their sweetness. The jammy onions coat the pasta so that the nori crisp really sticks to the noodles, adding delicate crunch and extra umami flavor.

2 tablespoons shallot oil (page 140), plus more for drizzling

2 medium yellow onions, thinly sliced

¼ teaspoon sea salt

12 ounces spaghetti pasta

1 tablespoon plus 1 teaspoon tamari

1 tablespoon balsamic vinegar

2 garlic cloves, grated

Sesame Nori Crisp (page 140), for sprinkling

Heat the shallot oil in a large, deep skillet over medium heat. Add the onions and salt and cook, stirring often, for 20 minutes, or until very soft and well browned.

Meanwhile, bring a large pot of salted water to a boil. Prepare the pasta according to the package instructions, cooking until al dente. Reserve 1 cup of the starchy pasta water, then drain.

Add the pasta, tamari, balsamic vinegar, and garlic to the skillet with the caramelized onions. Toss to combine, then add ¼ cup of the reserved pasta water, tossing and, if necessary, adding more pasta water, ¼ cup at a time, until the pasta is coated in a lightly creamy, glossy sauce. You might need all the pasta water or you might need slightly less.

Season to taste and toss again to make sure the pasta is well mixed with the onions. Serve topped with a drizzle of shallot oil and a generous sprinkle of sesame nori crisp.

SERVES **4** | **VEGAN** | **GLUTEN-FREE:** Use gluten-free Sesame Nori Crisp (page 140), gluten-free pasta, and certified gluten-free tamari.

ROOT VEGETABLE OKONOMIYAKI

WITH SESAME NORI CRISP

Jack and I first tried okonomiyaki on a trip to Japan nearly fifteen years ago, and we've loved it ever since. If you're not familiar with it, it's a Japanese savory pancake made with cabbage, scallions, and assorted meat or seafood. This recipe is a vibrant vegetarian twist. Instead of just cabbage, it features carrots, radishes, and pickled ginger for a bright pop of flavor. We always drizzle spicy mayo over the finished pancakes and generously sprinkle them with sesame nori crisp for a bit of crunch.

2½ cups shredded green cabbage

1½ cups julienned rainbow carrots (about 3 medium)

1 cup chopped scallions, plus more for garnish

1 cup thin watermelon radish matchsticks

⅓ cup pickled ginger, thinly sliced

1 cup all-purpose flour, spooned and leveled (see page 267)

2 teaspoons baking powder

1½ teaspoons sea salt

¾ teaspoon cane sugar

3 large eggs

¾ cup water

1½ teaspoons shallot oil (page 140), plus more for the pan

½ cup panko bread crumbs

Sesame Nori Crisp (page 140), for sprinkling

Microgreens, for garnish (optional)

Spicy Mayo

¼ cup mayonnaise

1 tablespoon sriracha

In a large bowl, toss together the cabbage, carrots, scallions, radishes, and pickled ginger.

In a medium bowl, whisk together the flour, baking powder, salt, and sugar.

In another medium bowl, whisk together the eggs, water, and shallot oil. Add the egg mixture to the flour mixture and mix until just combined. Pour the batter over the vegetable mixture and fold to combine, then fold in the panko.

Make the spicy mayo: In a small bowl, stir together the mayonnaise and sriracha.

Heat 1 teaspoon shallot oil in a nonstick skillet over medium heat. Scoop 1 cup of the batter into the skillet and use a spatula to flatten it into a 6-inch pancake, about ½ inch thick. Reduce the heat to medium-low and cook for 2 to 4 minutes per side, or until golden brown and cooked through. Repeat with the remaining batter, wiping out the skillet and adding 1 teaspoon shallot oil to the pan between batches.

To serve, top with the spicy mayo and sprinkle with sesame nori crisp. Garnish with scallions and microgreens, if using.

MAKES **5** *OR* **6** *PANCAKES*

CUCUMBER DAIKON SALAD

WITH SESAME NORI CRISP

Frying shallots used to intimidate me, but the method we use on page 141 for the sesame nori crisp has completely changed my fry game. Sure, it's an extra step compared to using store-bought fried onions, but you get a bonus gift in the process: shallot oil! In this refreshing salad, the shallot oil adds a wonderful toasty flavor to the creamy tahini-based dressing and pairs so well with the cucumber, daikon, and avocado. Tip: Be generous with the dressing so that the sesame nori crisp sticks to every bite.

½ English cucumber, chopped into ¾-inch pieces

6 ounces daikon radish, peeled and chopped into ¾-inch pieces

1 teaspoon fresh lemon juice, plus a lemon wedge for squeezing

¼ teaspoon sea salt

2 ripe but firm avocados, chopped into ¾-inch pieces

2 heaping tablespoons Sesame Nori Crisp (page 140)

Fresh cilantro leaves, for garnish

Sesame Shallot Dressing

¼ cup tahini

3 tablespoons water, plus more as needed

2 tablespoons fresh lemon juice

2 teaspoons maple syrup

¼ teaspoon sea salt

2 tablespoons shallot oil (page 140)

Place the cucumber and daikon in a medium bowl. Add the lemon juice and salt and toss to coat. Set aside while you make the dressing.

Make the sesame shallot dressing: In a medium jar, whisk together the tahini, water, lemon juice, maple syrup, and salt. Once well combined, whisk in the shallot oil. The dressing should have a creamy, drizzleable consistency. If it's too thick, add more water, 1 teaspoon at a time, as needed to loosen it.

Arrange the cucumber and daikon evenly on a serving platter. Add the avocado and squeeze lemon juice on top. Drizzle with about half the dressing, or enough to coat most of the vegetables. Sprinkle with the sesame nori crisp and garnish with cilantro. Season to taste and serve with the remaining dressing on the side.

SERVES **4** | **VEGAN** | **GLUTEN-FREE:** Use gluten-free Sesame Nori Crisp (page 140).

MORE WAYS TO USE

SESAME NORI CRISP

(AND THE BONUS SHALLOT OIL)

On the simplest tomato salad.

Arrange heirloom tomato slices on a platter and top with chopped scallions. Season with salt and a drizzle of shallot oil, then sprinkle with lots of sesame nori crisp.

Over eggs.

I love this nori crisp on eggs of all kinds—fried, soft-boiled, scrambled . . . Pro tip: If you're frying or scrambling eggs, cook them in shallot oil for oniony depth of flavor.

On roasted veggies with sesame shallot dressing.

The sesame shallot dressing on page 147 not only tastes amazing . . . it also helps the sesame nori crisp stick to any veggie you want to put it on! Some of my favorites are roasted cabbage wedges and roasted fall veggies like purple potatoes, Japanese sweet potatoes, and delicata squash.

On a juicy tomato sandwich.

Stir together a little mayo and white miso paste. Slather onto two slices of good bread, then top with thick tomato slices and sesame nori crisp.

On a cooling cucumber and watermelon salad.

Arrange chopped English cucumber, cubed watermelon, and diced avocado on a platter. Lightly drizzle with tamari and squeeze lime juice on top, then garnish with sesame nori crisp and fresh mint.

On a quick and easy rice bowl.

Perfect for a meal prep lunch or weeknight dinner! Top cooked rice (page 320) with a soft-boiled egg (page 321) or baked tofu (page 321 or store-bought), chopped scallions, thinly sliced radishes, and pickled ginger. Drizzle with spicy mayo (page 145) and sprinkle with sesame nori crisp!

COCONUT CURRY PEANUTS

Good luck making these peanuts and not eating them all straight off the baking sheet! They're seriously the best snack, but if you can contain yourself, keep them on hand to add a bright, curry-flavored crunch to dishes like lettuce wraps, salads, noodle bowls, and more.

- 1 cup unsalted peanuts
- 1 teaspoon melted coconut oil
- 1 teaspoon curry powder
- ½ teaspoon sea salt
- ¼ teaspoon cayenne pepper
- 1 cup unsweetened coconut flakes
- 2 teaspoons lime zest
- Pinch of red pepper flakes

YIELD: ABOUT **2** *CUPS*

VEGAN | GLUTEN-FREE

Preheat the oven to 350°F and line a baking sheet with parchment paper.

Place the peanuts on the baking sheet. Drizzle with the coconut oil and sprinkle with the curry powder, salt, and cayenne. Toss to coat and spread evenly on the baking sheet.

Bake for 8 to 10 minutes, or until the peanuts are lightly golden brown. Remove from the oven and toss with the coconut flakes. Bake for another 2 to 5 minutes, or until the coconut is lightly golden brown around the edges.

Remove from the oven. While the peanuts and coconut flakes are still warm, toss with the lime zest and red pepper flakes. Season to taste.

Let cool completely, then store in an airtight container at room temperature for up to 1 week.

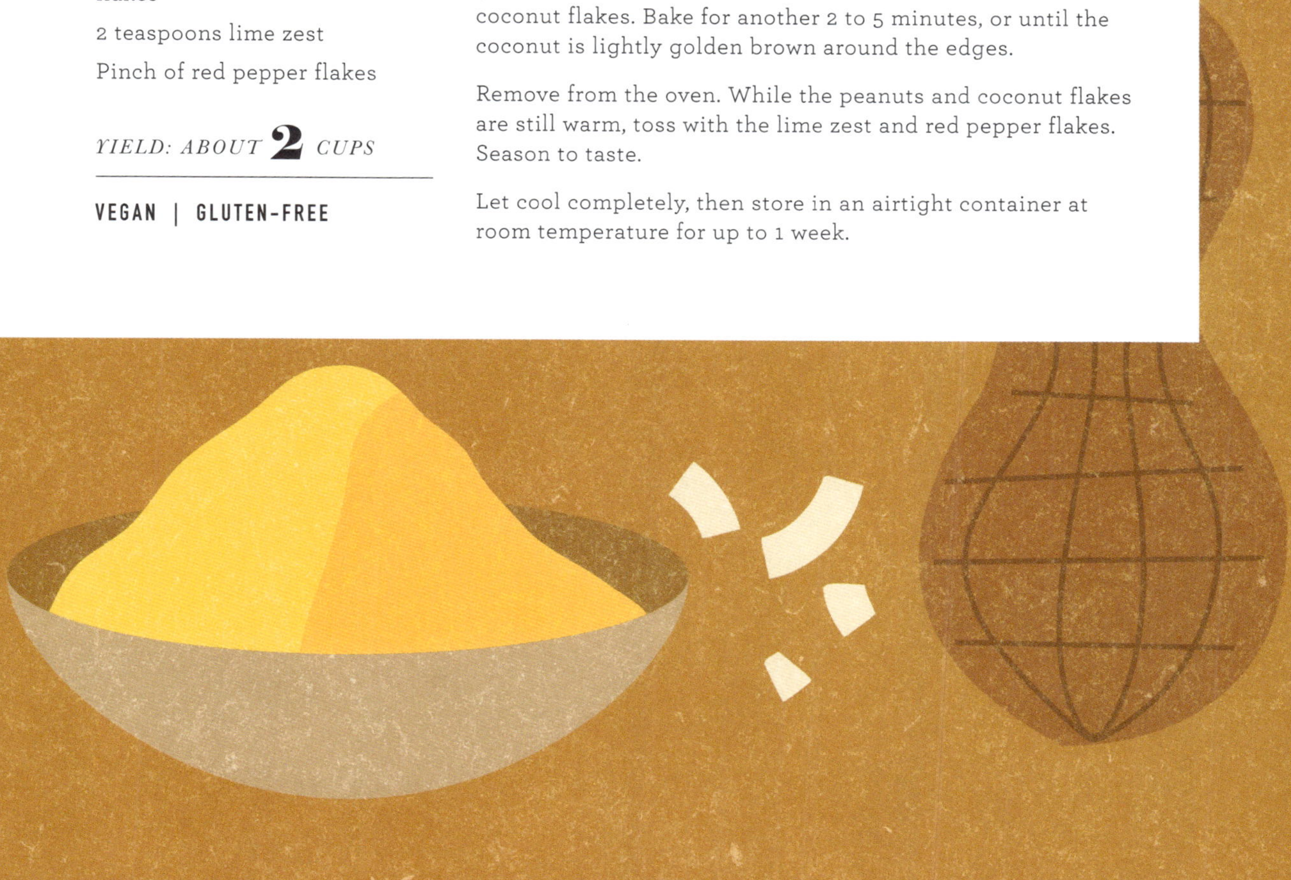

STICKY TOFU LETTUCE WRAPS

WITH COCONUT CURRY PEANUTS

It's always hard to choose favorite recipes in a cookbook. We like them all, or they wouldn't have made the cut! But as we test and retest each recipe, we end up with tons of leftovers. Every time we came back around to this one, the leftovers disappeared right away. So there you have it—a favorite. I love the mix of flavors and textures here. The sticky peanut sauce, with a little surprise chili crisp, is rich and savory, while the lettuce, radishes, and mint are super fresh. The crunchy coconut curry peanuts perfectly balance the soft tofu . . . You can probably see why these go quick!

14 ounces extra-firm tofu, patted dry and cut into ½-inch cubes

Avocado oil, for drizzling

Sea salt

2 tablespoons chopped scallions

1 head butter lettuce, leaves separated

½ cup radish matchsticks (about 3 red radishes or 1 small purple daikon)

½ cup Coconut Curry Peanuts (page 150)

Fresh mint leaves, for garnish

Lime wedges, for serving

Sticky Peanut Sauce

¼ cup creamy peanut butter

3 tablespoons rice vinegar

1½ tablespoons chili crisp

2 teaspoons honey or maple syrup

2 teaspoons tamari

2 teaspoons toasted sesame oil

1 teaspoon grated fresh ginger

Preheat the oven to 425°F and line a baking sheet with parchment paper.

Spread the tofu evenly on the baking sheet. Drizzle with avocado oil and sprinkle with salt. Bake for 20 minutes, or until the tofu is firm and browned around the edges.

Meanwhile, make the sticky peanut sauce: In a medium bowl, stir together the peanut butter, rice vinegar, chili crisp, honey, tamari, sesame oil, and ginger. The sauce will be fairly thick.

Remove the tofu from the oven and use tongs to toss with 3 tablespoons of the sauce until well coated. Spread evenly on the baking sheet and bake for 10 minutes, or until the tofu is lightly crisp and browned underneath.

Remove the tofu from the oven. Thin the remaining sauce with a little water, adding 1 teaspoon at a time as needed to reach a creamy, pourable consistency. Add the tofu and scallions and stir to coat.

Assemble the lettuce wraps. Layer two lettuce leaves for each wrap. Fill with some of the tofu mixture and radish matchsticks. Top with the coconut curry peanuts and garnish with mint. Serve with lime wedges.

SERVES **4** *AS AN APPETIZER* | **VEGAN** | **GLUTEN-FREE:** Use certified gluten-free tamari.

CRUNCHY SNAP PEA & NAPA CABBAGE SALAD

WITH COCONUT CURRY PEANUTS

How do you take a simple chopped cabbage salad and make it super fun? Add coconut curry peanuts! In this book, we often pair contrasting textures, but this recipe works because everything is crunchy or crisp. With the cabbage, snap peas, peanuts, and peppers, it's a crunchy party in a bowl! A light, refreshing peanut dressing ties it all together.

8 ounces snap peas

5 heaping cups shredded napa cabbage (from about 6 leaves)

1 Fresno chile or ¼ red bell pepper, stemmed and thinly sliced

2 scallions, chopped

½ cup chopped fresh cilantro, plus more for garnish

½ cup Coconut Curry Peanuts (page 150), plus more for garnish

Sea salt

Sweet Ginger Peanut Dressing

¼ cup fresh lime juice

3 tablespoons avocado oil

3 tablespoons creamy peanut butter

1 tablespoon maple syrup

1 tablespoon tamari

1 tablespoon toasted sesame oil

2 teaspoons grated fresh ginger

1 garlic clove, grated

Bring a large pot of water to a boil and set a bowl of ice water nearby. Drop the snap peas into the boiling water and blanch for 1 minute, or until crisp-tender and bright green. Use a slotted spoon or spider to scoop the snap peas out of the boiling water and into the ice water. Chill for at least 1 minute to stop the cooking process, then drain and pat dry with a kitchen towel. Chop into 1-inch pieces.

Make the sweet ginger peanut dressing: In a medium bowl, whisk together the lime juice, avocado oil, peanut butter, maple syrup, tamari, sesame oil, ginger, and garlic until smooth.

In a large bowl, toss the snap peas with the napa cabbage, Fresno chile, scallions, cilantro, and coconut curry peanuts. Drizzle with most of the dressing and toss to coat. Taste and add more dressing and/or salt as desired. Garnish with more cilantro and coconut curry peanuts and serve.

SERVES **4** *TO* **6** | **VEGAN** | **GLUTEN-FREE:** Use certified gluten-free tamari.

TIP

Treat these noodles as a blank canvas for any vegetables you like. Green beans, snap peas, or asparagus would work well in place of the broccoli (just adjust the cook time accordingly). Thinly sliced raw radishes, carrots, or cucumbers would also be delicious. You could even swap the edamame for tofu or another protein you prefer.

BROCCOLI MISO NOODLE BOWLS

WITH COCONUT CURRY PEANUTS

These noodles were made for busy weeknights. The trick? Everything—the noodles, broccoli, and spinach—cooks in the same pot of water, making the process super speedy with minimal dishes. The sweet and savory sauce is intentionally big on flavor so it can coat the noodles and season the veggies at the same time. (Note: A little goes a long way.) A sprinkle of coconut curry peanuts, sliced Fresno chile, and fresh herbs takes it over the top.

Miso Sauce

⅓ cup white miso paste
3 tablespoons avocado oil
3 tablespoons maple syrup
2 tablespoons fresh lime juice
2 tablespoons rice vinegar
1½ teaspoons sriracha
1 garlic clove, grated

For the Bowls

1 broccoli crown, cut into florets
5 ounces fresh spinach
8 ounces rice noodles
1½ cups frozen shelled edamame, thawed
1 cup Coconut Curry Peanuts (page 150)
1 Fresno chile, stemmed and thinly sliced
Fresh basil, mint, and/or cilantro, for garnish

Make the miso sauce: In a medium bowl, whisk together the miso, avocado oil, maple syrup, lime juice, rice vinegar, sriracha, and garlic. Set aside.

Make the bowls: Bring a large pot of water to a boil. Add the broccoli and cook for 2 minutes, or until bright green and tender but not mushy. Use a spider or slotted spoon to scoop the broccoli out of the boiling water and into a large bowl. Drain and transfer to a kitchen towel to dry. Repeat with the spinach, cooking for 30 seconds, or until just wilted.

Use the same pot of water to prepare the noodles according to the package instructions. Drain and rinse to prevent sticking, then transfer to a large bowl. Drizzle with half the miso sauce and toss to coat.

Portion the noodles into four bowls and evenly divide the broccoli, spinach, and edamame among them. Lightly drizzle with more of the miso sauce. Top with the coconut curry peanuts and Fresno chile. Garnish with fresh herbs and serve with the remaining sauce on the side.

SERVES **4** | VEGAN | GLUTEN-FREE

MORE WAYS TO USE

COCONUT CURRY PEANUTS

As a snack.

I can't stop munching on these when I have them in my kitchen!

On loaded sweet potato fries

topped with the turmeric yogurt sauce on page 125, Fresno chiles, scallions, and cilantro.

In a coconut rice bowl

topped with roasted shiitake mushrooms, the turmeric tofu on page 121, and the coconut mint sauce on page 205.

Over a sweet and savory noodle salad

made with strips of mango, red bell peppers, jalapeños, mint, and the sweet ginger peanut dressing on page 155.

On stuffed acorn squash

filled with lemony quinoa, apples, dried currants, and finely chopped parsley. Top it off with a dollop of the turmeric yogurt sauce on page 125.

On any simple stir-fry.

These curried peanuts provide an instant flavor boost! I love to pair them with stir-fried veggies like snow peas, bok choy, green beans, and/or bell peppers.

In fresh spring rolls

filled with rice noodles, baked tofu (page 321 or store-bought), bell pepper strips, cucumbers, basil, and mint. Serve with cilantro jalapeño sauce (page 231) or citrus serrano sauce (page 66) for dipping.

Over creamy pureed soups.

For contrasting crunch! Try them on the golden beet soup on page 101 or on a curried butternut squash soup.

SPICED ALMOND CRUNCH

Much like our coconut curry peanuts, these spiced almonds and sunflower seeds are just so darn snackable. Tamari, maple syrup, and smoked paprika give them a subtly sweet, smoky flavor. Crushed cumin and coriander seeds add earthy depth, while cayenne delivers a spicy kick. Give them a try—and if you've eaten them all before making it to the recipes in this chapter, go ahead and make another batch!

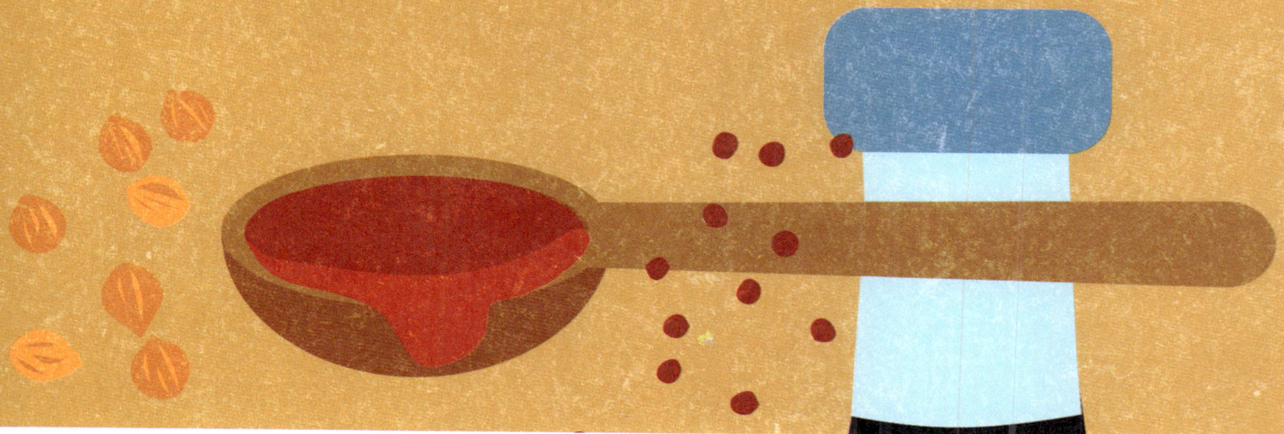

- 1½ cups raw almonds
- ¾ cup raw sunflower seeds
- 2 tablespoons tamari
- 1 teaspoon maple syrup
- 1 teaspoon whole coriander seeds, roughly crushed
- ½ teaspoon smoked paprika
- ½ teaspoon whole cumin seeds, roughly crushed
- ¼ teaspoon cayenne pepper

Preheat the oven to 350°F and line a baking sheet with parchment paper.

Place the almonds and sunflower seeds on the baking sheet. Drizzle with the tamari and maple syrup and sprinkle with the coriander seeds, smoked paprika, cumin seeds, and cayenne. Toss to coat and spread evenly on the baking sheet.

Bake for 14 to 18 minutes, or until dry and browned. Set aside for 10 minutes to crisp up.

Store in an airtight container at room temperature for up to 2 weeks.

YIELD: ABOUT **2½** *CUPS*

VEGAN | **GLUTEN-FREE:** Use certified gluten-free tamari.

LABNEH WITH LEMON HARISSA OIL

& SPICED ALMOND CRUNCH

I'm always looking for the next great crowd-pleasing appetizer. I get stuck in a rut of cheese boards, veggie dips, and hummus plates, all of which my regular guests have had plenty of. So last fall, I was excited to debut this labneh dip. It has everything: a creamy base, a drizzle of boldly spiced lemon oil, and a sprinkle of the spiced almond crunch. A touch of honey balances the spices, while fresh mint brightens it all up. I like to make the oil and almonds ahead of time so I can assemble it in minutes. And did my guests like it? Let's just say it disappeared so fast, we decided to double the recipe before publishing this book.

Labneh

2 cups whole milk Greek yogurt

½ teaspoon sea salt

Lemon Harissa Oil

⅓ cup extra-virgin olive oil

¼ teaspoon whole caraway seeds, crushed

¼ teaspoon whole coriander seeds, crushed

¼ teaspoon whole cumin seeds, crushed

1 teaspoon lemon zest

1 tablespoon spicy harissa

For Topping & Serving

Honey, for drizzling

½ cup Spiced Almond Crunch (page 160)

Fresh mint leaves

Pita

Fresh veggies

Make the labneh: In a medium bowl, stir together the yogurt and salt.

Scoop the mixture onto a layer of cheesecloth (or two layers, depending on the thickness of your yogurt). Bring the edges of the cheesecloth together, tie it around a wooden spoon, and place the spoon across the top of a medium bowl so that the labneh hangs in the center but does not touch the bottom of the bowl. Chill in the refrigerator overnight.

Make the lemon harissa oil: Heat the olive oil in a small skillet over medium heat. Add the caraway, coriander, and cumin seeds and cook for 15 seconds to 1 minute, or until fragrant. Remove from the heat and transfer to a heatproof bowl. Stir in the lemon zest, followed by the harissa.

To serve, remove the labneh from the cheesecloth. Transfer to a large plate and spread in an even layer. Top with drizzles of the lemon harissa oil and honey, then sprinkle with the spiced almond crunch and mint.

Serve with pita and veggies.

SERVES **6**

VEGAN: Use store-bought or homemade hummus (page 322) instead of labneh. Omit the honey.

GLUTEN-FREE: Use gluten-free Spiced Almond Crunch (page 160). Serve with gluten-free pita or crackers.

TIP

Making this salad ahead? Wait to add the spiced almond crunch and mint leaves until right before serving.

ISRAELI COUSCOUS CITRUS SALAD

WITH SPICED ALMOND CRUNCH

The secret to a great salad is combining as many contrasting elements as possible, and this one has it all—crunchy cucumbers, juicy orange segments, chewy dates, salty feta, and briny olives. And if that weren't enough, our spiced almond crunch takes it over the top. The crispy, spiced almond mixture plays perfectly against the chewy Israeli couscous, while the warm spices add wonderful depth. It packs up beautifully, so I love bringing it to gatherings or picnics. Try it once and it's bound to become part of your regular salad rotation.

1 cup uncooked Israeli couscous

2 tablespoons extra-virgin olive oil, plus more for drizzling

2 tablespoons fresh lemon juice

½ teaspoon lemon zest

1 garlic clove, grated

¼ teaspoon sea salt

3 Persian cucumbers, diced

1 cup mandarin orange segments (from about 3 mandarins)

2 soft Medjool dates, pitted and chopped*

¾ cup crumbled feta cheese

½ cup mixed olives, pitted and halved

¼ cup finely chopped fresh parsley

½ cup Spiced Almond Crunch (page 160), plus more for serving

⅓ cup fresh mint leaves

**If your dates are not soft, soak them in warm water for 5 to 10 minutes.*

Bring a medium pot of salted water to a boil. Prepare the couscous according to the package instructions, cooking until al dente. Drain and toss with a drizzle of olive oil to prevent sticking. Set aside to cool.

In a large bowl, whisk together the olive oil, lemon juice and zest, garlic, and salt. Add the cooked couscous, cucumbers, mandarin segments, dates, feta, olives, and parsley and toss to combine.

Season to taste and top with the spiced almond crunch and mint. Serve with more spiced almond crunch as desired.

SERVES **4**

VEGAN: Use vegan feta or skip the feta and increase the olive measurement to ¾ cup.

GLUTEN-FREE: Use gluten-free Spiced Almond Crunch (page 160). Use gluten-free couscous instead of regular, or replace it with brown rice (page 320).

ROASTED CAULIFLOWER WITH CITRUS TAHINI SAUCE

& SPICED ALMOND CRUNCH

Halfway through the winter, I'm pretty much done with comfort food, and I'm ready for something brighter. Something full of vibrant flavor that says sunshine is coming soon. Enter this roasted cauliflower dish! Nutty roasted cauliflower is drizzled with an orange-scented lemon tahini sauce, topped with pickled onions, and finished with our spiced almond crunch. The earthy spices add unexpected depth, and the crunch perfectly balances the creamy sauce.

1 large or 2 small cauliflowers (2¾ pounds)

Extra-virgin olive oil, for drizzling

Sea salt and freshly ground black pepper

¾ cup Spiced Almond Crunch (page 160)

¼ cup Pickled Onions (page 19)

⅓ cup fresh parsley leaves

Aleppo pepper

Citrus Tahini Sauce

¼ cup tahini

3 tablespoons fresh orange juice

2 tablespoons extra-virgin olive oil

2 tablespoons fresh lemon juice

1 teaspoon maple syrup

¼ teaspoon ground turmeric

¼ teaspoon sea salt

Preheat the oven to 450°F and line a baking sheet with parchment paper.

Remove any tough outer leaves from the cauliflower(s). If using two small cauliflowers, quarter them lengthwise. If using a large cauliflower, break it into large florets.

Place the cauliflower on the baking sheet. Drizzle with olive oil and sprinkle with salt and pepper. Use your hands to coat and spread evenly on the baking sheet. Roast for 30 to 35 minutes, or until the cauliflower is knife-tender and browned around the edges.

Meanwhile, make the citrus tahini sauce: In a medium bowl, stir together the tahini, orange juice, olive oil, lemon juice, maple syrup, turmeric, and salt. The sauce should have a creamy, drizzleable consistency. If it's too thick, add water, 1 tablespoon at a time, as needed to loosen it.

Transfer the cauliflower to a serving platter and drizzle generously with the sauce. Sprinkle with the spiced almond crunch, then top with the pickled onions and parsley. Sprinkle with Aleppo pepper, season to taste, and serve.

SERVES **4** | **VEGAN** | **GLUTEN-FREE:** Use gluten-free Spiced Almond Crunch (page 160).

MORE WAYS TO USE

SPICED ALMOND CRUNCH

As a snack.

Sometimes I make it just for snacking. :)

On green beans almondine 2.0.

Sauté fresh green beans with sliced shallot and garlic and squeeze lemon on them. Top with the crunch for an unexpected twist on the classic side dish!

On a green salad.

Don't feel like digging into a plain pile of lettuce? Sprinkle on the almond crunch for rich, savory flavor and, well . . . crunch! Pairs perfectly with the lemon vinaigrette on page 282.

On dressed-up cabbage.

Roast red cabbage wedges until they're tender and charred. Top with the lemon yogurt on page 105, fresh mint or parsley, and generous sprinkles of the crunch.

In a nutty wild rice pilaf.

Perfect for your Thanksgiving table or any fall meal. Toss cooked wild rice with olive oil, roasted sweet potatoes or carrots, red onion, fresh rosemary, and dried cranberries. Top with the crunch.

On creamy pureed soups.

Just like the coconut curry peanuts (page 150), this almond crunch is a great soup topper. You could use it on the golden beet soup on page 101 or the celery root soup on page 223!

In a packable grain salad

made with cooked farro (page 320), roasted broccoli and cauliflower, big crumbles of feta, and an apple cider vinegar dressing.

On caramelized roasted carrots.

Spread a swoosh of the lemon yogurt on page 105 on a serving platter. Top with roasted carrots, drizzles of the chimichurri on page 67, and sprinkles of the crunch. Roasted beets or winter squash would be great here too!

CRUNCHY VEGGIE

SLAWS

Radishes

Fennel

Cabbage

Carrots

Broccoli stems

CUT VEGGIES INTO STRIPS TO GET 4 CUPS

EXTRAS: apple matchsticks | jalapeño or bell pepper matchsticks | thinly sliced fresno chiles | orange juice and/or zest | honey or maple syrup | fresh herbs | fresh ginger

MIX & MATCH

Any crunchy vegetable can become a flavorful slaw! Start with 4 cups crunchy veg, then choose an acid, something oniony, and something creamy for a quick, crispy topping for sandwiches, bowls, and more. Round it out with extras like apples for sweetness, chiles for heat, and/or herbs for fresh flavor.

ADD 2 TABLESPOONS ACID

Choose:

Apple cider vinegar

Rice vinegar

Fresh lemon juice

Fresh lime juice

Toss in something oniony

Choose:

2 scallions, chopped

1 cup thinly sliced red onion

¼ cup chopped fresh chives

Season to taste with ½ to 1 teaspoon sea salt

MAKE IT CREAMY

Choose:

¼ cup whole milk Greek yogurt + 2 tablespoons mayo

¼ cup peanut butter

2 tablespoons tahini + 1 tablespoon olive oil *(add an extra 1 to 2 tablespoons acid too!)*

For vinegar slaw

Skip a creamy component and add 1 tablespoon olive oil and an additional 1–2 tablespoons acid.

A FEW GOOD COMBOS:

1. **Creamy Apple Ranch Slaw (page 173)**
2. **Tahini Broccoli Stem Slaw (page 175)**
3. **Colorful Citrus Slaw (page 177)**
4. **Jalapeño Peanut Slaw (page 179)**

BBQ TOFU BOWLS

WITH CREAMY APPLE RANCH SLAW

As a vegetarian-ish person who lived in Austin for a long time, I've eaten a lot of coleslaw. Here's how it goes: family comes to town, everyone wants BBQ, and Jeanine eats coleslaw. Two servings for me, please. I'm not mad about it—I actually love coleslaw that much. In fact, it inspired me to make this saucy veg BBQ bowl based on a really fun, flavorful, ranch-forward slaw. The slaw is sweet (thanks to the apples), crunchy, and creamy. It's delicious with the saucy tofu. Hot sauce and dill pickles take these bowls over the top!

32 ounces high-protein tofu, patted dry and cut into 1-inch cubes

1 cup BBQ sauce

3 cups cooked rice (page 320)

2 avocados, sliced

½ cup chopped dill pickles

Chopped fresh chives

Sea salt

Hot sauce, for serving

Creamy Apple Ranch Slaw

2 cups shredded green cabbage

1 cup shredded red cabbage

1 cup carrot matchsticks

1 medium apple, cut into thin matchsticks

¼ cup chopped fresh chives

¼ cup whole milk Greek yogurt

2 tablespoons mayonnaise

2 tablespoons apple cider vinegar

1 teaspoon Dijon mustard

1½ teaspoons onion powder

1 teaspoon garlic powder

½ teaspoon dried dill

½ teaspoon sea salt

Preheat the oven to 450°F and line a baking sheet with parchment paper.

Place the tofu on a plate and brush with some of the BBQ sauce, flipping to coat all sides. Arrange evenly on the baking sheet.

Bake for 20 minutes, or until browned around the edges. Flip, brush with more BBQ sauce, and bake for 5 minutes, or until well browned.

Meanwhile, make the creamy apple ranch slaw: In a large bowl, toss together the green and red cabbage, carrots, apple, and chives. Add the yogurt, mayonnaise, apple cider vinegar, mustard, onion powder, garlic powder, dried dill, and salt. Toss until well coated. Season to taste and chill in the refrigerator until ready to serve.

Remove the tofu from the oven and brush with more BBQ sauce. Assemble bowls with the rice, BBQ tofu, slaw, avocado, pickles, and chives. Season to taste with salt and serve with hot sauce.

SERVES **4** *TO* **6**

VEGAN: Replace the Greek yogurt and mayonnaise with vegan mayo. Omit the salt from the slaw and season to taste before serving.

GLUTEN-FREE

HIPPIE VEGGIE SANDWICH

WITH TAHINI BROCCOLI STEM SLAW

In *Simple Feel Good Food*, there's a broccoli melt sandwich with pickled broccoli stems that's one of my favorite recipes in the book. The crunchy pickles were such a delight, and I loved how they used a part of the vegetable that usually gets thrown away. This sandwich takes a different approach—it's cold, it's fresh—but I love it just as much. This time, I toss sliced broccoli stems with scallions, lemon juice, and creamy tahini to create a bright, nutty slaw that balances rich slices of avocado and feta. I hope you make both recipes and feel inspired to hang on to those broccoli stems!

Tahini Broccoli Stem Slaw

4 cups broccoli stem matchsticks

1 cup tiny broccoli florets

2 scallions, chopped

¼ cup fresh lemon juice

2 tablespoons tahini

1 tablespoon extra-virgin olive oil

1 teaspoon honey

½ teaspoon sea salt

For the Sandwiches

8 slices soft grainy bread

Mayonnaise or store-bought or homemade hummus (page 322)

1 (8-ounce) block feta cheese, sliced into ⅛-inch-thick planks

2 avocados, sliced

Microgreens

Make the tahini broccoli stem slaw: In a large bowl, toss together the broccoli stem matchsticks, broccoli florets, and scallions. Add the lemon juice, tahini, olive oil, honey, and salt and toss until well coated. Chill in the refrigerator for 30 minutes to allow the vegetables to soften and the flavors to meld.

Assemble the sandwiches: Slather the bread slices with mayonnaise or hummus. Top four of the slices with the feta planks followed by the avocado slices, a generous scoop of the slaw, and microgreens. Top with the remaining bread slices, slice each sandwich in half, and serve.

MAKES **4** *SANDWICHES*

VEGAN: Use maple syrup instead of honey. Replace the feta with baked tofu (page 321 or store-bought) or the turmeric tofu on page 121.

GLUTEN-FREE: Use gluten-free bread.

TIP

Make your slaw extra-colorful by using a mix of different types of radishes! Green, pink, and purple daikon; watermelon radishes; and red radishes are all great here.

PINTO BEANS

WITH COLORFUL CITRUS SLAW

A simple bowl of well-cooked, nicely seasoned pinto beans is something I'll happily eat for dinner any night of the week. They're humble but nourishing and oh-so-comforting. Though they aren't quick to make, most of the cook time is hands-off—and afterward you'll have beans for the week! To jazz them up and make a more complete meal, I pair them with a crunchy citrus slaw that complements their creamy texture and earthy flavor.

2 cups dry pinto beans

2 tablespoons extra-virgin olive oil

½ medium white onion, diced

1 jalapeño pepper, stemmed and diced

2 garlic cloves, chopped

1 teaspoon ground cumin

6 cups water, plus more as needed

1½ teaspoons sea salt

½ teaspoon dried oregano

Freshly ground black pepper

2 tablespoons fresh lime juice, plus wedges for serving

2 serrano peppers, stemmed and thinly sliced

Crumbled cotija cheese, for garnish

Fresh cilantro, for garnish

Colorful Citrus Slaw

3 cups radish matchsticks

1 cup carrot matchsticks

2 scallions, chopped

2 tablespoons fresh lime juice

1 tablespoon fresh orange juice

1 tablespoon extra-virgin olive oil

2 teaspoons orange zest

1 teaspoon lime zest

1 teaspoon honey

½ teaspoon sea salt

Place the beans in a large colander. Rinse well and transfer to a large bowl. Cover with 2 to 3 inches of water and discard any beans that float. Soak at room temperature for 8 hours or overnight. Drain and rinse.

Heat the olive oil in a large pot or Dutch oven over medium heat. Add the onion and jalapeño and cook, stirring occasionally, for 5 minutes, or until softened.

Stir in the garlic and cumin, then add the beans, water, 1 teaspoon of the salt, the oregano, and several grinds of pepper. Bring to a boil, then reduce the heat to maintain a simmer. Simmer, stirring occasionally, until the beans are tender and the cooking liquid is thick. I like to check mine starting at 1 hour and every 15 minutes after that, usually cooking them for 1½ to 2 hours total. The exact timing will depend on the freshness of your beans. Add more water to the pot as needed if the beans start to dry out.

Meanwhile, make the colorful citrus slaw: In a large bowl, toss together the radishes, carrots, and scallions. Add the lime juice, orange juice, olive oil, orange zest, lime zest, honey, and salt and toss until well coated. Season to taste.

Remove the beans from the heat and stir in the lime juice and remaining ½ teaspoon salt. Season to taste and portion into bowls. Top with the slaw, serrano slices, cotija, and cilantro. Serve with lime wedges.

SERVES **4** *TO* **6**

VEGAN: Use maple syrup instead of honey. Skip the cotija or replace it with vegan feta.

GLUTEN-FREE

CHARRED SWEET POTATOES

WITH JALAPEÑO PEANUT SLAW

How do you take simple, soft sweet potatoes and transform them into an exciting, textural meal? Give them a good char and add a flavorful slaw! Roasting the sweet potatoes with honey and lime juice is a game changer—the edges become crisp and caramelized, and the potatoes take on a wonderful tang. And then there's the slaw: this one is a creamy, Asian-inspired peanut slaw with lots of fresh mint. Serve this as a meal on its own or on a platter as a vibrant vegetable side.

3 medium or 4 small sweet potatoes (2 pounds), roll-cut into large chunks

Avocado oil, for drizzling

1½ teaspoons fresh lime juice

1½ teaspoons honey

Sea salt

Toasted sesame oil, for drizzling

½ cup toasted peanuts or Coconut Curry Peanuts (page 150)

Fresh mint leaves, for garnish

Lime wedges, for serving

Jalapeño Peanut Slaw

2 cups radish matchsticks

1 cup shredded green cabbage

1 cup shredded red cabbage

2 jalapeño peppers, stemmed, seeded, and cut into thin matchsticks

2 scallions, chopped

¼ cup creamy peanut butter

2 tablespoons rice vinegar

½ teaspoon toasted sesame oil

¾ teaspoon sea salt

½ cup chopped fresh cilantro

½ cup fresh mint leaves

Preheat the oven to 450°F and line a large baking sheet with parchment paper.

Place the sweet potatoes on the baking sheet. Drizzle with avocado oil, the lime juice, and honey and sprinkle with salt. Toss to coat and spread evenly on the baking sheet. Roast for 30 to 40 minutes, or until tender and charred underneath.

Meanwhile, make the jalapeño peanut slaw: In a large bowl, toss together the radishes, green and red cabbage, jalapeños, and scallions. Add the peanut butter, rice vinegar, sesame oil, and salt and toss until well coated. Add the cilantro and mint and toss to combine. Season to taste and chill in the refrigerator until ready to serve.

Divide the charred sweet potatoes among four plates. Add a scoop of the slaw to each and top with a drizzle of sesame oil, the peanuts, and mint. Serve with lime wedges.

SERVES **4**

VEGAN: Use maple syrup instead of honey.

GLUTEN-FREE

CHAPTER 4

BASIL | DILL

MINT | SAGE

MORE HERBS WE LOVE

HERBY

How do you upgrade a dish with just one ingredient? Add a fresh herb! Each one brings its own special qualities to the table, so I've organized this chapter by type. Start with sweet basil or earthy sage . . . and then venture on to citrusy shiso or anise-like tarragon. Their bold, fresh flavors will blow you away!

BASIL

For me, the minute a leaf of basil hits a fat slab of juicy, perfectly ripe tomato (with a sprinkle of flaky sea salt) is the moment I feel like I've made it in life. I've survived yet another cold Chicago winter, and I can hardly believe the warm sun is touching my skin, another summer is here, and a tomato can actually taste good again.

Of course, tomatoes aren't the only thing made better by basil. I challenge you to think of any summer-produce dish that isn't improved by a sprinkle of this herb—salads, pastas, sandwiches . . . check, check, check. Tomatoes, zucchini, yellow squash, eggplant . . . Whatever you're making, just add basil!

SUMMER ON A PLATE SALAD

WITH BASIL WHIPPED FETA

I wrote this in my first book and I'll write it again here—I don't think there's any food more perfect than a ripe peach. This recipe is for that point in the summer when peaches are at peak sweetness and heirloom tomatoes are available in every size, shape, and color. The fruit does the talking in this salad, so we gently supported it with a swoosh of creamy basil whipped feta underneath and finished it with a shower of fresh basil on top.

Basil Whipped Feta

4 ounces feta cheese

½ cup whole milk Greek yogurt

2 tablespoons extra-virgin olive oil

1 tablespoon fresh lemon juice

1 small garlic clove

1½ cups fresh basil leaves

For the Salad

3 medium colorful heirloom tomatoes (1¼ pounds), sliced into ½-inch wedges

2 peaches, pitted and sliced into ½-inch wedges

½ cup red and yellow cherry tomatoes, halved

Extra-virgin olive oil, for drizzling

Flaky sea salt

Freshly ground black pepper

Fresh basil leaves, for garnish

Edible flowers, for garnish (optional)

Make the basil whipped feta: Crumble the feta into a food processor. Add the yogurt, olive oil, lemon juice, and garlic and pulse until smooth and creamy. Add the basil and pulse to combine, stopping when the sauce has green flecks.

Assemble the salad: Spread the whipped feta in a thin layer on a large plate or serving platter. Top with the heirloom tomatoes, peaches, and cherry tomatoes. Drizzle with olive oil and sprinkle with flaky sea salt and several grinds of pepper. Garnish with fresh basil and edible flowers, if using. Season to taste and serve immediately.

SERVES **4** *TO* **6**

VEGAN: Replace the basil whipped feta with the basil whipped tofu on page 322.

GLUTEN-FREE

ULTIMATE HEIRLOOM TOMATO SANDWICH

WITH BASIL MISO SPREAD

From July through September, I eat a tomato sandwich every day for lunch. It's the kind that's best eaten over the kitchen sink while the juices run down your arms. It's simple and perfect—a ripe tomato, a slather of good mayo, sprinkles of flaky sea salt, and a few fresh basil leaves. Since you don't need a recipe for that, we came up with this creamy basil spread (to replace the mayo) that makes this tomato sandwich truly ultimate. It combines blended cashews with tofu for a luxe creamy texture and has a secret dab of miso for umami flavor. Make a batch and keep it in your fridge for tomato sandwiches all week!

Basil Miso Spread

1 cup raw cashews

½ cup crumbled extra-firm tofu

½ cup water

3 tablespoons fresh lemon juice

2 tablespoons extra-virgin olive oil

1 tablespoon white miso paste

1 garlic clove

½ teaspoon sea salt

½ cup fresh basil leaves

For the Sandwich

2 slices sourdough bread

Sliced colorful heirloom tomatoes

Flaky sea salt

Arugula

Fresh basil leaves

Make the basil miso spread: In a high-speed blender, place the cashews, tofu, water, lemon juice, olive oil, miso, garlic, and salt. Blend until smooth and creamy. Add the basil and briefly blend until the sauce has green flecks. Season to taste and chill until ready to use.

Assemble the sandwich: Slather the bread slices with the basil miso spread. Top one with tomato slices. Season with flaky sea salt, then top with arugula, basil, and the second slice of bread. Slice in half and serve.

Store leftover basil miso spread in an airtight container in the refrigerator for up to 5 days.

SERVES **1** *WITH EXTRA BASIL MISO SPREAD*

VEGAN

GLUTEN-FREE: Use gluten-free bread.

CREAMY YELLOW SQUASH GNOCCHI

WITH BASIL

I love to make pasta sauces out of every vegetable under the sun. Anything from carrots to greens to eggplants can turn into a luscious hidden-vegetable sauce. Blended yellow squash creates the creamy gnocchi sauce in this recipe. Some white beans are hiding in there as well (protein!), but what's not hiding is the basil. Pulsed in and showered on top, it brightens up this bowl of summer comfort food.

2 tablespoons extra-virgin olive oil, plus more for drizzling

1 shallot, thinly sliced (⅓ cup)

2 garlic cloves, thinly sliced

2 medium yellow squash (1 pound), sliced into thin rounds or half-moons

½ teaspoon sea salt

Freshly ground black pepper

1 (16- to 17.5-ounce) package store-bought gnocchi

½ cup cooked white beans, drained and rinsed (page 320)

1½ tablespoons fresh lemon juice

1 tablespoon white miso paste

2 tablespoons chopped fresh basil, plus ½ cup torn basil leaves for garnish

1 tablespoon toasted pine nuts

Heat 1 tablespoon of the olive oil in a large skillet over medium heat. Add the shallot, garlic, yellow squash, salt, and several grinds of pepper. Cook, stirring occasionally, for 6 to 8 minutes, or until the squash is soft.

Bring a large pot of salted water to a boil. Prepare the gnocchi according to the package instructions, cooking until they float. Reserve 1 cup of the gnocchi cooking water, then drain. Toss the gnocchi with a drizzle of olive oil to prevent sticking.

Transfer half the squash mixture to a blender. Add the beans, the remaining 1 tablespoon olive oil, the lemon juice, miso, and ½ cup of the gnocchi water. Blend until smooth. Add the chopped basil and briefly blend until the sauce has green flecks.

Pour the sauce into the skillet with the remaining yellow squash. Add the gnocchi and stir to coat, adding more gnocchi water as needed to create a creamy sauce.

Season to taste. Top with a drizzle of olive oil, the torn basil, and pine nuts and serve.

SERVES **3** *OR* **4**

VEGAN

GLUTEN-FREE: Use certified gluten-free gnocchi.

MORE WAYS TO USE

FRESH BASIL

In pesto.

Obvious, but oh-so-good. Find my recipe on page 66.

In a frosty strawberry smoothie.

Strawberries + basil are a match made in heaven! Blend together frozen strawberries, banana, a handful of basil, and your milk of choice for a refreshing summer drink.

In a pesto vinaigrette.

Thin pesto with more olive oil and white wine vinegar to create a bold, herbaceous dressing for any summer salad.

In a fun, fruity salsa.

Use basil instead of cilantro in the peach salsa on page 205. If you like, replace the peaches with another summer fruit, like nectarines or strawberries!

On any pizza.

Pull your homemade pie out of the oven, then shower it with fresh basil.

In a Thai-inspired green curry.

Simmer chopped eggplant, green beans, extra-firm tofu, and a sprig of basil (or better yet, Thai basil) in coconut milk with a spoonful of green curry paste. Serve over cooked rice (page 320), with more basil on top and lime wedges on the side.

In herb-infused drinks.

Make the minty simple syrup on page 309 with basil instead of mint. Use in cocktails, mocktails, or homemade lemonade!

DILL

If you don't like dill, you might want to skip over this section—or, better yet, give dill a chance! Fun fact: My sister didn't like dill until she started getting it in her CSA box and learned that fresh dill is delicious, especially when it's paired with the right ingredients. Of course, my co-author Phoebe and I (herb lovers through and through) consider dill the ultimate spring herb, and we use it unapologetically in the following recipes—with seasonal produce like asparagus, leeks, and carrots, as well as dill-loving staples like eggs, rice, potatoes, and feta.

ASPARAGUS EGGS BENEDICT

WITH CREAMY TARRAGON DILL SAUCE

I love eggs Benedict, but after making this recipe, I'll never order it at a restaurant again. This sauce isn't just lighter than a traditional hollandaise—it's also so much more flavorful because, in my opinion, eggs need herbs. Specifically, dill, tarragon, and chives go exceptionally (or egg-ceptionally?) well with eggs, especially when served over sautéed asparagus and a toasted English muffin. This is my perfect spring brunch.

Creamy Tarragon Dill Sauce

½ cup mayonnaise

½ cup whole milk Greek yogurt

1 tablespoon fresh lemon juice

1 teaspoon Dijon mustard

¼ teaspoon ground turmeric

3 tablespoons finely chopped fresh tarragon

2 tablespoons finely chopped fresh chives

2 tablespoons finely chopped fresh dill

For the Eggs Benedict

Extra-virgin olive oil, for drizzling

1 bunch asparagus, trimmed and chopped into 2-inch pieces

Sea salt and freshly ground black pepper

Lemon wedge, for squeezing

4 large eggs

1 tablespoon white wine vinegar

Unsalted butter, for spreading

2 English muffins, halved and toasted

Chopped fresh dill, for garnish

Make the creamy tarragon dill sauce: In a medium bowl, stir together the mayonnaise, yogurt, lemon juice, mustard, and turmeric. Add the tarragon, chives, and dill and stir to combine. The sauce should have a creamy, drizzleable consistency. If it's too thick, add water, 1 tablespoon at a time, as needed to loosen it. Season to taste and chill in the refrigerator until ready to serve.

Make the eggs Benedict: Heat a drizzle of olive oil in a large skillet over medium heat. Add the asparagus and season with salt and pepper. Cook, stirring often, for 3 to 6 minutes, or until tender. Remove from the heat and squeeze lemon juice over the asparagus.

Poach the eggs. Crack the eggs into four separate small bowls or ramekins. Bring a medium pot of water to a gentle boil. Add the vinegar and stir the water so that it moves in a circular motion. Gently drop the eggs into the water, give the water another gentle stir, and cook for 3½ to 4 minutes. Use a slotted spoon to scoop the eggs out of the water.

Butter the English muffin halves and evenly divide the sautéed asparagus among them. Top each with a poached egg. Drizzle with the creamy tarragon dill sauce. Garnish with dill and season with several grinds of pepper.

SERVES **2** *TO* **4**

GLUTEN-FREE: Use gluten-free English muffins.

POTATO LEEK BAKED POTATO

WITH LOTS OF DILL

This recipe is a delicious mashup of two potato-y favorites: potato leek soup and a crispy-skinned baked potato! I sauté fresh leeks until they're soft and jammy, then mix them with dill, lemon juice, and Dijon mustard for a bright, tangy kick. Then I stuff them into baked potatoes with feta, lemon yogurt sauce, and MORE fresh dill to create a loaded-potato situation that's anything but boring. It's fresh and lively enough to serve in spring but so cozy and comforting that you'll crave it in fall and winter too.

4 medium russet potatoes

¼ cup extra-virgin olive oil, plus more for the potatoes

2 pounds leeks (about 3 medium), white and light green parts only, halved lengthwise, washed well, and thinly sliced

½ teaspoon sea salt, plus more for sprinkling

Freshly ground black pepper

2 garlic cloves, grated

½ cup chopped fresh dill, plus more for garnish

1 tablespoon fresh lemon juice

1 teaspoon Dijon mustard

½ cup crumbled feta cheese

Yogurt Sauce

¾ cup whole milk Greek yogurt

1 tablespoon fresh lemon juice

Heaping ¼ teaspoon onion powder

Heaping ¼ teaspoon sea salt

Preheat the oven to 425°F and line a baking sheet with parchment paper.

Use a fork to poke a few holes in the potatoes. Place on the baking sheet, rub with olive oil, and sprinkle liberally with salt all over. Bake for 45 to 60 minutes, or until the potatoes are fork-tender and the skin is crisp.

Meanwhile, make the yogurt sauce: In a medium bowl, stir together the yogurt, lemon juice, onion powder, and salt. The yogurt should have a creamy, dollopable consistency. If it's too thick, add water, 1 teaspoon at a time, as needed to loosen it. Chill in the refrigerator until ready to serve.

Heat the olive oil in a large skillet over medium heat. Add the leeks, salt, and several grinds of pepper. Cook, stirring often, for 15 minutes, or until the leeks are soft and jammy. Reduce the heat to low as needed to prevent the leeks from browning. Stir in the garlic and remove from the heat. Stir in the dill, lemon juice, and mustard.

Slice open the baked potatoes and fluff the insides. Scoop out 3 tablespoons of the fluffy insides from each potato and save for another use. Sprinkle the insides of the potatoes with salt and pepper, then fill with the leek mixture and feta. Top with a dollop of the yogurt sauce and garnish with dill and several grinds of pepper. Serve with the remaining yogurt sauce on the side.

SERVES **4**

GLUTEN-FREE

CRISPY FETA CARROT BOWLS

WITH DILL PISTACHIO PESTO

Meet my go-to spring grain bowls! They star a bright, bold dill pistachio pesto that gets used two ways: some is stirred into the rice for seasoning and the rest is served as a sauce on the side. Roasted carrots, pickled onions, and crispy nuggets of roasted feta take these over the top.

1 bunch medium carrots (about 12 ounces), trimmed and halved lengthwise

8 ounces feta cheese, roughly torn into ½- to 1-inch pieces

1½ cups cooked chickpeas, drained, rinsed, and patted dry (page 320)

Extra-virgin olive oil, for drizzling

Sea salt and freshly ground black pepper

3 cups cooked rice (page 320)

4 soft Medjool dates, pitted and chopped*

⅓ cup Pickled Onions (page 19)

2 tablespoons crushed toasted pistachios

Chopped fresh dill, for garnish

Fresh parsley leaves, for garnish

Dill Pistachio Pesto

1 cup fresh dill

1 cup fresh parsley

¼ cup shelled raw pistachios

2 tablespoons fresh lemon juice, plus another 1 tablespoon for the rice

1 garlic clove

¼ teaspoon sea salt, plus another ¼ teaspoon for the rice

½ cup extra-virgin olive oil

**If your dates are not soft, soak them in warm water for 5 to 10 minutes.*

Preheat the oven to 425°F and line two baking sheets with parchment paper.

Place the carrots on one side of one of the baking sheets and the feta on the other side. Place the chickpeas on the second baking sheet. Drizzle all three with olive oil and sprinkle the carrots and chickpeas with salt and pepper. Toss to coat and spread evenly on the baking sheets. Roast the carrots and feta for 15 to 25 minutes, or until the carrots are fork-tender and the feta is crisp and browned. Roast the chickpeas for 20 to 30 minutes, or until crisp.

Meanwhile, make the dill pistachio pesto: In a food processor, place the dill, parsley, pistachios, 2 tablespoons lemon juice, the garlic, and ¼ teaspoon salt. Pulse until finely chopped. With the food processor running, drizzle in the olive oil and pulse until well combined.

Measure ⅓ cup of the pesto and set it aside for serving. Stir the remaining pesto into the rice along with the remaining 1 tablespoon lemon juice and ¼ teaspoon salt. Season to taste.

Assemble bowls with a scoop of the rice, the roasted carrots, crispy feta, chickpeas, dates, and pickled onions. Sprinkle with the crushed pistachios, garnish with dill and parsley, and serve.

SERVES **4** | **VEGAN:** Skip the feta. | **GLUTEN-FREE**

MORE WAYS TO USE

FRESH DILL

In homemade dill pickles.

Prepare the brine for the pickled onions on page 19. Fill a lidded jar with a few dill sprigs, sliced Persian cucumbers, and smashed garlic. Cover with the brine, chill overnight, and store in the fridge for up to 2 weeks!

In a tangy feta pasta

with lemon and spinach. Toss your favorite short pasta with lots of crumbled feta, a big squeeze of lemon juice, sautéed spinach, and dill (or the dill pistachio pesto on page 199).

On all things asparagus.

Top oven-roasted asparagus with a generous sprinkle of dill and crumbled feta, or make a spring salad with blanched asparagus, chopped cucumbers, chickpeas, capers, and dill. Drizzle with the tahini green goddess on page 66.

In a creamy kohlrabi slaw.

Follow the template on page 170, using kohlrabi matchsticks, lemon juice, yogurt + mayo, and thinly sliced red onion. Add toasted sunflower seeds and lots of dill!

In egg or potato salad.

Dill is my favorite part of mayo-dressed salads like these. Add plenty of the fresh stuff, plus chopped dill pickles for good measure!

In a bright beet salad.

Toss chopped roasted beets with the lemon vinaigrette on page 282. Add lots of fresh dill, toasted walnuts, and feta or goat cheese.

MINT

I was going to give you a pep talk about how easy mint is to grow and how hard it is to mess up. But as I sit here looking out my window, I see a pot with about ten photo-worthy leaves and the rest a crunchy mess. Another year, I made the mistake of planting two varieties in the same pot, and—if you know mint—you know how that went: badly. The year before that, I had mint growing everywhere, and we drank mojitos every night.

So I'll skip the gardening advice and just share a few of my favorite mint recipes. Whether you're clipping it from your own plant or picking it up at the store, I hope these inspire you with some fresh flavor.

TIP

Make a few of the components ahead of time. I like to prep the salsa and the mint sauce up to 1 day in advance. That way, it's super simple to assemble the bowls when we're ready to eat.

PEACH SALSA HALLOUMI BOWLS

WITH COCONUT MINT SAUCE

This recipe is my kind of summer meal—one that's fresh and flavorful but still plenty satisfying. It starts with a base of rice and black beans. Then I pile on grilled halloumi, a scoop of peach salsa, and creamy avocado slices. A handful of fresh mint leaves and drizzles of mint sauce are the perfect finishing touches!

Coconut Mint Sauce

2 cups fresh cilantro

2 cups fresh mint leaves, plus more for garnish

½ cup unsweetened coconut yogurt

2 tablespoons fresh lime juice

2 teaspoons avocado oil

2 teaspoons grated fresh ginger

1 small garlic clove

1 teaspoon cane sugar

½ teaspoon sea salt

Peach Salsa

2 to 3 ripe peaches, pitted and diced (2 cups)

½ cup diced red bell pepper

¼ cup chopped fresh cilantro

¼ cup diced red onion

½ jalapeño pepper, stemmed and finely diced

Juice and zest of 1 lime

¼ teaspoon sea salt

For the Bowls

8 ounces halloumi cheese, sliced into ½-inch-thick planks

Avocado oil, for drizzling

3 cups cooked rice (page 320)

1½ cups cooked black beans, drained and rinsed (page 320)

2 avocados, sliced

RECIPE CONTINUES

Make the coconut mint sauce: In a food processor, place the cilantro, mint, coconut yogurt, lime juice, avocado oil, ginger, garlic, sugar, and salt. Pulse until combined. Season to taste.

Make the peach salsa: In a medium bowl, mix together the peaches, red bell pepper, cilantro, red onion, jalapeño, lime juice and zest, and salt. Season to taste.

Prepare the bowls: Preheat a grill or grill pan to high heat. Place the halloumi on a large plate. Drizzle with avocado oil and rub both sides with your hands to coat. Place the halloumi on the hot grill and reduce the heat to medium. Grill for 2 to 3 minutes per side, or until well charred.

Assemble bowls with the rice, black beans, halloumi, and avocado. Top with scoops of the peach salsa and drizzle with the mint sauce. Garnish with mint leaves. Season to taste and serve with the remaining mint sauce on the side.

SERVES **4**

VEGAN: Skip the halloumi.

GLUTEN-FREE

CURRIED POTATO EGG BAKE

WITH PEA & MINT CHUTNEY

This curried egg bake is kind of like a frittata, but it's a step above the throw-together type I usually make on Sunday mornings with random leftover veggies. It's so good that I'd actually suggest making it for dinner. The curried potato filling provides the perfect base for the flavorful pea and mint chutney, which isn't just dolloped on—it's piled high. The chutney is fresh and minty, with a spicy kick from ginger and jalapeños. To streamline the recipe, you can roast the potatoes or make the chutney ahead of time.

3 medium Yukon Gold or yellow potatoes (1 pound)

8 large eggs

3 tablespoons all-purpose flour

1 teaspoon baking powder

2 tablespoons avocado oil, plus more for the potatoes

½ medium yellow onion, chopped

1¼ teaspoons sea salt, plus more for sprinkling

Freshly ground black pepper

1 jalapeño pepper, stemmed and diced

2 garlic cloves, chopped

1½ teaspoons curry powder

Stems from 1 bunch fresh cilantro, finely chopped, plus ¼ cup cilantro leaves for garnish

¼ cup fresh mint leaves, for garnish

1 Fresno chile, stemmed and thinly sliced, for garnish (optional)

Pea & Mint Chutney

1 cup frozen peas, thawed

½ jalapeño pepper, stemmed and roughly chopped

2 tablespoons fresh lemon juice

1 small garlic clove

1 (½-inch) piece fresh ginger, peeled and roughly chopped

¼ teaspoon sea salt

1 cup fresh mint leaves

¼ cup avocado oil

RECIPE CONTINUES

Preheat the oven to 400°F and line a baking sheet with parchment paper.

Use a fork to poke a few holes in the potatoes. Place on the baking sheet, rub with avocado oil, and sprinkle liberally with salt all over. Bake for 45 to 60 minutes, or until fork-tender.

Allow the potatoes to cool slightly. When they are cool enough to handle, roughly tear the skins and crumble the flesh. Set aside.

Meanwhile, make the pea and mint chutney: In a food processor, place the peas, jalapeño, lemon juice, garlic, ginger, and salt. Pulse until well chopped. Add the mint and pulse to combine. With the food processor running, drizzle in the avocado oil and pulse until well combined. Season to taste and chill in the refrigerator until ready to serve.

Make the egg bake. In a large bowl, beat the eggs. Add the flour and baking powder and whisk until combined. A few lumps in the mixture are okay.

Heat the avocado oil in a 10-inch oven-safe skillet over medium heat. Add the onion, salt, and several grinds of pepper and cook, stirring occasionally, for 4 to 6 minutes, or until softened. Stir in the jalapeño, garlic, and curry powder, then add the potatoes and cilantro stems and stir to combine.

Pour the egg mixture into the pan and shake it to distribute. Use a spatula to lightly mix the eggs with the potatoes in places, bringing some potato pieces up to the surface.

Transfer to the oven and bake for 15 to 20 minutes, or until the eggs are set.

Spoon the chutney into the center of the egg bake. Garnish with the mint, cilantro leaves, and Fresno chile, if using. Slice and serve.

SERVES **8**

MY FAVORITE SUMMER COCKTAIL

WITH BLUEBERRY MINT SHRUB

I have my friend Megan to thank for introducing me to this blueberry shrub—and to shrubs in general. If you're not familiar, a shrub is a syrup made by steeping vinegar with fruit and sugar. Megan makes a wonderful one with local blueberries and lavender from her garden, and I tried it in a cocktail when I was at her house one summer evening. Judging by its pink color, I thought the cocktail would be overly sweet, but as I sipped it, I found that the punch of the apple cider vinegar mixed with the floral essence of the lavender was actually incredibly refreshing. Because fresh lavender can be hard to come by, I make this version using fresh mint, and it's every bit as delicious. Try the shrub in this gin cocktail, or make a simple mocktail by mixing it with sparkling water. Either way, you'll have a perfect summer drink.

Blueberry Mint Shrub

1 cup blueberries

1 cup apple cider vinegar

½ cup cane sugar

½ cup fresh mint leaves

For the Cocktail

1½ ounces gin or aquavit

Ice

2 ounces sparkling water

Fresh mint leaves, for garnish

Make the blueberry mint shrub: In a small bowl, muddle the blueberries. Transfer to a large lidded jar and add the apple cider vinegar, sugar, and mint. Cover and shake to combine, then chill in the refrigerator for 2 days.

Strain the shrub to remove the blueberries and mint, then transfer the liquid to another lidded jar. Store in the refrigerator for up to 2 weeks.

Make the cocktail: Add 1½ ounces of the shrub, the gin, and a few ice cubes to a mixing glass. Stir until chilled. Strain into a chilled cocktail glass and top with the sparkling water.

Garnish with mint leaves and serve.

SERVES **1** *WITH EXTRA BLUEBERRY MINT SHRUB* | VEGAN | GLUTEN-FREE

MORE WAYS TO USE

FRESH MINT

In a shaved fennel salad

with lots of lemon and fresh fruit. Try one with peaches in the summertime and oranges or grapefruit in the winter!

In an abundant spring pasta.

Toss fresh mint leaves with your favorite short pasta, sautéed asparagus and radishes, crumbled feta, and the lemon vinaigrette on page 282.

In a quick summer grain bowl

with cooked quinoa or bulgur, chopped tomatoes and cucumbers, roasted chickpeas, Pickled Onions (page 19), and Red Pepper Tahini (page 24) or Eggplant Yogurt Sauce (page 34).

On a refreshing noodle bowl

with baked tofu (page 321 or store-bought), julienned cucumbers, pickled ginger, and the sweet ginger peanut dressing on page 155.

On a colorful grilled vegetable platter.

For a showstopping summer side dish, drizzle grilled eggplant, peppers, and zucchini with the mint pesto on page 66. Add more fresh mint leaves for garnish!

SAGE

Once October hits, everyone goes crazy for all things pumpkin and squash. I'm on board too, but I'd add a few more to that list: celery root, sweet potatoes, and the real hero of fall flavor—sage.

For me, sage is a sense memory of waking up on Thanksgiving morning to the smell of my mom prepping the holiday meal. It's an herb that carries the cozy feeling of togetherness, and all I have to do to re-create that is start cooking with it. As soon as sage hits the pan or starts roasting in the oven—before I've even taken a bite—fall has officially begun.

HOT HONEY HASSELBACK BUTTERNUT SQUASH

WITH CRISPY SAGE

When I need an impressive veg-forward dish to serve as the centerpiece of a holiday meal, I turn to this recipe. Butternut squash is softened, then sliced and drizzled with a hot honey dressing that seeps in and caramelizes the edges of the squash as it cooks. The sage between the slices becomes wonderfully crisp, and its savory flavor balances perfectly with the sweetness of the squash. The first time I served it at my family's Christmas dinner, it was all anyone could talk about!

1 small to medium butternut squash (about 1 pound 10 ounces), peeled, halved lengthwise, and seeded

Extra-virgin olive oil, for drizzling

Sea salt and freshly ground black pepper

30 to 40 fresh sage leaves

2 tablespoons chopped toasted walnuts

2 tablespoons crumbled feta cheese

Hot Honey Ginger Dressing

2 tablespoons apple cider vinegar

2 tablespoons extra-virgin olive oil

1 tablespoon honey

½ garlic clove, grated

½ teaspoon grated fresh ginger

¼ teaspoon red pepper flakes

⅛ teaspoon sea salt

Freshly ground black pepper

Preheat the oven to 425°F and line a baking sheet with parchment paper.

Place the squash halves on the baking sheet. Drizzle with olive oil and sprinkle with salt and pepper. Use your hands to coat. Roast cut side down for 15 to 20 minutes, or until the squash begins to soften.

Make the hot honey ginger dressing: In a medium bowl, whisk together the apple cider vinegar, olive oil, honey, garlic, ginger, red pepper flakes, salt, and several grinds of pepper.

When the squash is cool enough to handle, place one half cut side down on a cutting board. Lay butter knives or chopsticks along both of its long ends. Use a sharp knife to cut the squash crosswise into ¼-inch-thick slices, stopping when your knife reaches the butter knives or chopsticks so that the squash stays intact at the bottom. Repeat with the other squash half.

RECIPE CONTINUES

Use a large spatula to carefully transfer both squash halves back to the baking sheet. Drizzle with 1 to 2 tablespoons of the dressing, or enough to moisten the surface of the squash. Allow the dressing that slides off the squash to pool around it on the baking sheet. Roast for 30 minutes.

Place the sage leaves in a small bowl and toss with a drizzle of olive oil. Remove the squash from the oven and carefully slide the sage leaves into the cracks between the squash slices, placing one in every one or two slices. Roast for another 10 to 15 minutes, or until the squash is tender and the sage is crisp.

Use a large spatula to carefully transfer the squash to a serving platter. Drizzle with more dressing and top with the walnuts and feta. Season to taste and serve with the remaining dressing on the side.

SERVES **2** *AS A MAIN OR* **4** *AS A SIDE*

VEGAN: Skip the feta or use vegan feta. Use maple syrup instead of honey.

GLUTEN-FREE

TIP

Like the shallot oil on page 140, the leftover sage oil is great for cooking! Store it in an airtight container or jar at room temperature for up to 2 weeks. Use it to add sage-y flavor to other dishes, like the baked sweet potato pasta on the following page.

CREAMY CELERY ROOT SOUP

WITH SAGE SALSA VERDE

If there was an "ugly veggie" contest, celery root would surely win. But if there was a blindfolded "most delicious fall vegetable" award? I bet celery root would be ranked up there with butternut squash—it just doesn't get the same love. But we love it! This simple blended celery root soup is creamy like potato soup, but better, with a hint of celery flavor, but better. Drizzles of fried sage salsa verde lift and brighten the whole thing up.

2 tablespoons extra-virgin olive oil

1 medium yellow onion, chopped

¾ teaspoon sea salt

Freshly ground black pepper

5 cups peeled and chopped celery root (about 2 medium-large)

2 garlic cloves, chopped

4 cups vegetable broth

1½ cups cooked white beans, drained and rinsed (page 320)

1 tablespoon fresh lemon juice

Toasted pine nuts, for garnish

Sage Salsa Verde & Sage Oil

1 cup vegetable oil

½ cup fresh sage leaves

½ cup finely chopped fresh parsley

1 garlic clove, grated

1 teaspoon white wine vinegar

Heat the olive oil in a large pot or Dutch oven over medium heat. Add the onion, salt, and several grinds of pepper and cook, stirring occasionally, for 5 to 8 minutes, or until softened. Add the celery root and garlic and cook, stirring, for 2 minutes. Add the broth and beans. Cover and simmer for 30 to 35 minutes, or until the celery root is tender.

Meanwhile, make the sage salsa verde and sage oil: Place a fine-mesh strainer over a heatproof bowl. In a small saucepan, combine the vegetable oil and sage leaves. Cook over medium heat until the oil begins to bubble, then cook, stirring occasionally, for 3 to 5 minutes, or until the sage leaves become speckled and start to crisp up. Quickly remove the pan from the heat and pour the sage leaves and oil into the strainer set over the bowl.

Spread the sage leaves on a paper towel–lined plate and set them aside for 5 minutes to crisp up.

Finely chop the fried sage and place it in a small bowl. Add the parsley, garlic, vinegar, and ¼ cup of the reserved sage oil and stir to combine.

Allow the soup to cool slightly and transfer to a blender, working in batches if necessary. Add the lemon juice and blend until smooth. If the soup is too thick, add water, ¼ cup at a time, as needed to reach your desired consistency. Season to taste and serve topped with the sage salsa verde, pine nuts, and a drizzle of sage oil.

SERVES **4** *TO* **6** | VEGAN | GLUTEN-FREE

STAUB
STAUB

BAKED SWEET POTATO RICOTTA PASTA

WITH SAGE

If it's October and you've just opened this book, this is the recipe you should make first. It's the most comforting way I can think of to celebrate fall flavors. Sweet potatoes get blended with ricotta to create a luscious sauce, and the bonus sage oil from the previous recipe (page 223) adds that cozy, crisp-air, leaves-are-falling magic. (No sage oil? No problem—this pasta is still fantastic without it.)

2 medium sweet potatoes

1 cup water

¼ cup plus 2 tablespoons sage oil (page 223) or extra-virgin olive oil, plus more for drizzling

1 tablespoon balsamic vinegar

3 garlic cloves

Pinch of nutmeg

1¼ cups whole milk ricotta cheese

1¼ teaspoons sea salt

12 ounces short pasta

½ medium yellow onion, chopped

Freshly ground black pepper

½ cup fresh sage leaves, half chopped, half left whole

1½ cups grated Gruyère cheese

Preheat the oven to 425°F and line a baking sheet with parchment paper.

Use a fork to poke a few holes in the sweet potatoes. Place on the baking sheet and roast for 45 to 60 minutes, or until fork-tender.

When the sweet potatoes are cool enough to handle, measure 1¼ cups of the soft flesh and transfer to a blender. Add the water, ¼ cup of the sage oil, the balsamic vinegar, garlic, nutmeg, ½ cup of the ricotta, and ¾ teaspoon of the salt. Blend until smooth.

Bring a large pot of salted water to a boil. Prepare the pasta according to the package instructions, cooking until al dente. Reserve ½ cup of the starchy pasta water, then drain.

Heat the remaining 2 tablespoons sage oil in a 10-inch oven-safe skillet over medium heat. Add the onion, the remaining ½ teaspoon salt, and several grinds of pepper. Cook, stirring occasionally, for 5 to 8 minutes, or until softened. Stir in the chopped sage and cook for 1 minute. Remove from the heat and add the pasta, sauce, and ¼ cup of the reserved pasta water. Stir to combine, adding more pasta water as needed to create a creamy sauce.

Dollop the pasta with the remaining ¾ cup ricotta and top with the Gruyère and whole sage leaves. Drizzle with sage oil, making sure to get some on each of the sage leaves.

Bake for 20 to 25 minutes, or until the cheese is browned and the sage leaves are crisp.

SERVES **4**

GLUTEN-FREE: Use gluten-free pasta.

MORE WAYS TO USE

FRESH SAGE

On crispy potatoes.

Drizzle the sage salsa verde on page 223 over crispy smashed or roasted potatoes.

In a hearty lentil salad.

Toss cooked green lentils (page 321) with sage salsa verde (page 223). Fold in roasted sweet potatoes and shallots or red onion.

In brown butter pasta sauce.

When you're browning butter, add a few sage leaves to the pan a minute or two before the butter is fully browned so that the leaves crisp up and infuse the butter with flavor. Toss the butter with your favorite pasta.

In cozy fall and winter soups.

Add a tablespoon of chopped fresh sage to a butternut squash soup, sweet potato soup, white bean soup, or lentil soup near the start of the cooking process. You could even use sage instead of rosemary in the chunky veggie soup on page 235!

On holiday-worthy delicata squash.

Spread lemon ricotta (page 71) on a serving platter. Top with roasted delicata squash, toasted pecans, a drizzle of honey, and spoonfuls of sage salsa verde (page 223).

In stuffing.

My favorite part of Thanksgiving dinner!

MORE HERBS WE LOVE

I could have written a whole book about herbs, with a dedicated chapter for each and every type. That might have to be a book for another time and place, but for now, suffice it to say—I love all herbs. In this section, I wanted to highlight some that I haven't covered yet. For example, shiso and Thai basil are two of my favorite summer herbs (I grow mine on my back deck; they're also available at Asian markets year-round). Rosemary and thyme are staples in my fall and winter cooking. I should also note that parsley and cilantro didn't get their own chapters because, well, flip to nearly any recipe in this book and you'll find a way to use one or the other.

SHISO SPRING ROLLS

WITH CILANTRO JALAPEÑO SAUCE

I wanted to include shiso in this book because it's one of my favorite herbs. If you've never tried it, you can think of it like a cross between basil and mint, with hints of cumin, clove, and citrus. I love the flavor it brings to these fresh spring rolls, although if you can't find it, don't worry—you can simply use basil and mint. These are rolled up with tofu, cucumber, avocado, and pickled ginger for a sweet pop. The cilantro jalapeño sauce has a little kick, which contrasts with the freshness of these rolls without overpowering the herbs' delicate flavor.

Cilantro Jalapeño Sauce

3 jalapeño peppers, stemmed and chopped

¼ cup fresh cilantro

2 scallions, roughly chopped

1 tablespoon grated fresh ginger

1 tablespoon rice vinegar

1½ teaspoons cane sugar

¼ teaspoon sea salt

½ cup avocado oil

For the Spring Rolls

8 ounces rice vermicelli noodles

8 large rice paper spring roll wrappers

2 cups loosely packed fresh shiso, basil, and/or mint leaves

7 ounces baked tofu (page 321 or store-bought), cut into strips

2 Persian cucumbers, peeled into ribbons

1 avocado, sliced

½ purple daikon radish (3 ounces), thinly sliced on a mandoline

⅓ cup pickled ginger

Make the cilantro jalapeño sauce: In a blender, place the jalapeños, cilantro, scallions, ginger, rice vinegar, sugar, and salt. Blend until combined. With the blender running on low, drizzle in the avocado oil and blend until smooth. Season to taste and chill in the refrigerator until ready to serve.

Make the spring rolls: Bring a large pot of water to a boil. Prepare the noodles according to package instructions. Drain and rinse under cold water.

Fill a large bowl with warm water and dampen a clean kitchen towel. Spread the kitchen towel over a flat work surface.

Soak one of the spring roll wrappers in the warm water for 15 seconds, or until pliable. Lay the wrapper flat on the kitchen towel and place some of the herbs, noodles, tofu, cucumber, avocado, daikon, and pickled ginger in the center. Fold the sides of the wrapper over the fillings and roll tightly to close. Repeat with the remaining spring roll wrappers and fillings.

Serve with the cilantro jalapeño sauce for dipping.

SERVES **2** *AS A MAIN OR* **4** *AS AN APPETIZER* | **VEGAN** | **GLUTEN-FREE**

ONE-POT TORTELLINI WITH ASPARAGUS

& TARRAGON

Some of my best ideas come when I'm short on time. I first made this pasta for dinner on a spring night when I came home from the farmers market with asparagus, peas, fresh herbs . . . and a screaming baby. In an effort to make dinner as quickly as possible, I threw the veggies and fresh packaged tortellini into the same pot of boiling water since they all cook in around 3 minutes. This one-pot boil saved me time and energy by not dirtying any extra pans. After draining, I tossed it all in a lemon vinaigrette and added lots of tarragon and other fresh herbs, which elevated the whole dish. Super simple and satisfying, this one has been in our family rotation ever since!

Lemon Vinaigrette

¼ cup extra-virgin olive oil

¼ cup fresh lemon juice

1 garlic clove, grated

1 teaspoon Dijon mustard

½ teaspoon sea salt

¼ teaspoon dried thyme

Freshly ground black pepper

For the Tortellini

2 (9-ounce) packages fresh cheese tortellini

1 bunch asparagus, trimmed and chopped into 1-inch pieces

1½ cups fresh or frozen peas

½ cup fresh tarragon leaves

⅓ cup toasted pine nuts

Zest of 1 lemon

Pinch of red pepper flakes

Freshly ground black pepper

Shaved pecorino cheese, for garnish

Fresh dill, minced chives, mint leaves, and/or microgreens, for garnish

Make the lemon vinaigrette: In a medium bowl, whisk together the olive oil, lemon juice, garlic, mustard, salt, thyme, and several grinds of pepper.

Make the tortellini: Bring a large pot of salted water to a boil. Add the tortellini, asparagus, and peas and cook for 2 to 4 minutes, or until the asparagus is crisp-tender but still bright green and the tortellini is cooked through.

Drain and transfer to a large bowl. Drizzle with the vinaigrette and toss. Add the tarragon, pine nuts, lemon zest, red pepper flakes, and several grinds of pepper and toss again.

Season to taste and top with shaved pecorino and fresh herbs and/or microgreens. Serve with more pecorino, if desired.

SERVES **4**

VEGAN: Use vegan tortellini and skip the cheese.

CHUNKY VEGGIE SOUP

WITH ROSEMARY & PARSLEY

I'm a summer person through and through, but once October hits, even I can't deny that the farmers market is in its most magical state. In Chicago, it's also the last month for the outdoor markets, so you can bet that every time I go, I stock up—actually, I stockpile. Squash, potatoes, carrots, onions, hearty herbs like rosemary . . . I buy way too much, and then I make this soup on repeat. Full of chunky fall veggies, it's a hearty soup that I love for dinner, served with good crusty bread.

2 tablespoons extra-virgin olive oil

1 pound leeks (about 1 large or 2 medium), white and light green parts only, halved lengthwise, washed well, and chopped

4 lacinato kale leaves, stems finely diced, leaves torn

1½ teaspoons sea salt

Freshly ground black pepper

4 garlic cloves, chopped

1 tablespoon finely chopped fresh rosemary leaves

3 medium carrots, chopped on the bias into 1-inch pieces

2 medium Yukon Gold or yellow potatoes, chopped into 1-inch pieces

1 delicata squash, halved lengthwise, seeded, and chopped into 1-inch pieces

Stems from 1 bunch fresh parsley, bundled, plus parsley leaves for garnish

4 cups vegetable broth

2 cups water

2 tablespoons apple cider vinegar

Freshly grated Parmesan or pecorino cheese, for serving (optional)

Heat the olive oil in a large pot or Dutch oven over medium heat. Add the leeks, kale stems, 1 teaspoon of the salt, and several grinds of pepper and cook, stirring occasionally, for 5 to 8 minutes, or until softened. Add the garlic and rosemary and cook, stirring, for 1 minute.

Add the carrots, potatoes, squash, parsley stem bundle, broth, water, apple cider vinegar, and the remaining ½ teaspoon salt. Cover and simmer, stirring occasionally, for 30 to 35 minutes, or until the potatoes and carrots are tender.

Uncover and remove the parsley stem bundle. Stir in the kale leaves, cover, and simmer for 5 minutes. Season to taste and serve topped with parsley and Parmesan, if desired.

SERVES **6**

VEGAN: Skip the cheese.

GLUTEN-FREE

10 THINGS TO MAKE WHEN YOU HAVE MANY HERBS

1 A green sauce!

Green goddess dressing (page 66) and pesto (page 66) are my go-to ways to use up a variety of soft, leafy herbs.

Best herbs to use: basil, chives, cilantro, dill, mint, parsley, tarragon

2 A salad.

I almost never make a salad without an herb (or two or three or four) in it. Toss soft, leafy herbs into a simple green salad for unexpected depth, or use them in grain salads, beans salads, tomato salads, and more.

Best herbs to use: basil, chives, cilantro, dill, mint, parsley, shiso, tarragon, thyme

3 Roasted vegetables.

Infuse extra flavor into a tray of roasted vegetables by tossing them with finely chopped woody herbs before roasting. Or roast them with herb sprigs on top.

Best herbs to use: rosemary, sage, thyme

4 Compound butter.

Stir minced herbs into softened butter (add a pinch of salt too, if your butter isn't salted). Wrap in parchment and refrigerate until firm, then use on potatoes, sweet potatoes, biscuits, cornbread, grits, and more.

Best herbs to use: chives, dill, rosemary, sage, thyme

5 An omelet.

Chopped or torn soft, leafy herbs are such a simple, delicious omelet filling! Kick things up another notch by adding goat cheese, feta, or avocado.

Best herbs to use: basil, chives, dill, tarragon

6 A sandwich.

We're used to piling lettuce on sandwiches—why not herbs? Anything soft and leafy will add a burst of freshness to your next sandwich or wrap.

Best herbs to use: basil, cilantro, dill, mint, parsley, shiso, tarragon

7 Homemade vegetable broth.

Add an herb or two to a pot of vegetable broth, and you won't believe how flavorful it is! *Tip:* Even just herb *stems* can add a ton of flavor. I often use the leaves in other dishes and then freeze the stems until I'm ready to make stock. Waste not, want not!

Best herbs to use: parsley, rosemary, thyme

8 A many-veggie pasta.

Toss your favorite short pasta with a mix of blanched, sautéed, or roasted veggies. Finish it with a squeeze of lemon juice, a drizzle of olive oil, and a shower of soft, leafy herbs. A little cheese like Parmesan or feta wouldn't hurt either.

Best herbs to use: basil, chives, dill, mint, parsley, tarragon, thyme

9 A noodle bowl.

I love tossing cold noodles with a zesty dressing and a pile of leafy herbs. I often make a quick dressing with rice vinegar, tamari, toasted sesame oil, and ginger. The sweet ginger peanut dressing on page 155 is a favorite too.

Best herbs to use: basil, cilantro, mint, shiso

10 Soup.

Most soup recipes start with sautéing an onion or other allium. Add chopped woody herbs at the same time. They'll make any pot of soup taste extra-cozy and comforting!

Best herbs to use: rosemary, sage, thyme

CHAPTER 5

CAPERS
PICKLED SWEET CORN
SLOW-ROASTED TOMATOES
KIMCHI
FIVE ESSENTIAL LEMON RECIPES

TANGY

In case it isn't obvious, I love lemons. I also love all kinds of tangy things—kimchi, capers, pickled veggies . . . I've always described what they add to a dish as "a bright pop of flavor," and I don't think there's a better way to say it. They bring acidity and lightness that pep up the rest of the plate.

CAPERS

There was a time when I didn't like capers—or rather, I thought I didn't. I can't even remember why. A trip to Southern Italy changed my mind, maybe because the capers were better there, but probably because I would never dare ask an Italian for an ingredient substitute. Since then, they've become a staple in my cooking. I love them in lemony salad dressings, in tomato dishes, and especially as a way to bring briny depth to Caesar dressings and tartar-like sauces.

TIP

Use a Meyer lemon if you can find one! It'll add a sweeter, almost floral taste to this dish.

LEMONY BAKED HALLOUMI WITH TOMATOES

& CAPERS

This is a dish I started making often in the summer because I always have an abundance of cherry tomatoes (see page 56 to find out why). I also love how it comes together in a single baking dish, making it relatively hands-off and minimizing cleanup.

Unlike the baked feta trend that went viral on TikTok, the cheese here doesn't get mixed in. Instead, it stays intact as the main protein—think white fish fillets. Meanwhile, the tomatoes burst in the oven, the lemon slices soften, and the capers add bright, briny flavor to the juices that collect at the bottom of the dish. Serve with crusty bread to soak it all up.

1 pint cherry tomatoes

1 (8-ounce) block halloumi cheese, halved lengthwise to create two thin slabs

1 small organic lemon, thinly sliced and seeded

2 garlic cloves, thinly sliced

2 tablespoons capers

1 tablespoon extra-virgin olive oil, plus more for brushing

2 tablespoons pine nuts

2 tablespoons shelled raw pistachios

Freshly ground black pepper

Red pepper flakes

Fresh basil leaves, for garnish

Crusty bread, for serving

Preheat the oven to 400°F and brush an 8×8-inch or similar baking dish with olive oil.

Sprinkle some of the cherry tomatoes at the bottom of the baking dish. Nestle the halloumi slabs among them, placing them cut side down. Top with half the lemon slices, then the garlic and capers, followed by the remaining tomatoes and lemon slices. Drizzle with the olive oil and bake for 25 to 30 minutes, or until the tomatoes are soft and bursting.

Meanwhile, toast the nuts. Place the pine nuts and pistachios in a small dry skillet over medium-low heat. Toast for 1 to 2 minutes, or until fragrant. Remove from the pan and roughly chop.

Remove the baking dish from the oven. Season the baked halloumi with several grinds of pepper and sprinkle with the chopped toasted nuts and red pepper flakes. Garnish with basil.

Season to taste and serve with crusty bread.

SERVES **4**

GLUTEN-FREE: Serve with gluten-free bread.

TIP

Follow the instructions on page 170 to make a quick slaw with cabbage, red onion, lemon juice, and olive oil. Pile it onto the sandwiches for freshness and crunch!

CRISPY CAULIFLOWER SANDWICHES

WITH LEMON CAPER MAYO

This sandwich is my take on a fried chicken or fish sandwich—but instead of meat, it features ever-versatile cauliflower. For contrast, I top the crispy cauliflower slabs with a creamy lemon caper mayo.

1 medium cauliflower (about 2 pounds)
1½ cups panko bread crumbs
1 tablespoon smoked paprika
2 teaspoons garlic powder
2 teaspoons onion powder
2 teaspoons sea salt
2 large eggs
Extra-virgin olive oil, for drizzling
4 brioche buns, for serving
Cabbage Slaw (page 170)
Pickles, for serving (optional)

Lemon Caper Mayo

½ cup mayonnaise
¼ cup whole milk Greek yogurt
1 tablespoon chopped fresh chives
2 teaspoons capers, chopped
1 teaspoon fresh lemon juice
½ teaspoon Dijon mustard
½ garlic clove, grated

Preheat the oven to 425°F and line a large baking sheet with parchment paper.

Remove any tough outer leaves from the cauliflower, then slice the cauliflower into 1-inch-thick slabs. Slices from the center will stay intact and form "steaks," while outer slices will fall apart into florets. Cut the steaks in half through the core to form two slabs. Trim the edges of the florets to form two flat sides.

On a rimmed tray, mix together the panko, smoked paprika, garlic powder, onion powder, and salt. In a shallow bowl, beat the eggs. Dip the cauliflower slabs and florets into the egg, then coat with the panko mixture. Arrange evenly on the baking sheet. Drizzle generously with olive oil and bake for 30 to 40 minutes, or until knife-tender, crispy, and golden brown.

Make the lemon caper mayo: In a small bowl, stir together the mayonnaise, yogurt, chives, capers, lemon juice, mustard, and garlic.

Assemble sandwiches on the buns with a generous slather of the mayo, a cauliflower slab or several florets, a scoop of slaw, and pickles, if using.

SERVES **4** *WITH EXTRA CAULIFLOWER*

VEGAN: Replace the eggs with 2½ tablespoons ground flaxseed mixed with ½ cup water; let stand for 5 minutes before breading the cauliflower. Use vegan buns and vegan lemon caper mayo (page 322).

GLUTEN-FREE: Use gluten-free panko and gluten-free buns.

BROCCOLI SHEET PAN CAESAR

WITH CAPER CAESAR-ISH DRESSING

Caesar salad lovers, this recipe is for you! A Caesar-inspired sheet pan meal, it's totally not traditional, but it still captures all the tangy, briny flavors that make the classic so craveable. You'll toss fresh romaine and a creamy, caper-flecked dressing with roasted broccoli and chickpeas. The best part? Parmesan and panko roast alongside the chickpeas and broccoli in the oven, essentially forming Parmesan crisps as they bake.

1½ cups cooked chickpeas, drained, rinsed, and patted dry (page 320)

1 tablespoon capers

Sea salt

2 broccoli crowns (about 1 pound), cut into small florets

½ cup panko bread crumbs

1½ teaspoons extra-virgin olive oil, plus more for drizzling

1 cup freshly grated Parmesan cheese

3 cups chopped romaine lettuce (about 3 large leaves)

Caper Caesar-ish Dressing

½ cup mayonnaise

3 tablespoons tahini

2 tablespoons fresh lemon juice

2 teaspoons caper brine

1½ teaspoons capers, chopped

1 teaspoon Dijon mustard

1 garlic clove, grated

Freshly ground black pepper

Preheat the oven to 425°F and line a large baking sheet with parchment paper.

Place the chickpeas and capers on the baking sheet. Drizzle with olive oil, sprinkle lightly with salt, and toss to coat. Spread evenly on the baking sheet and roast for 5 minutes.

Place the broccoli in a large bowl. Drizzle with olive oil, sprinkle lightly with salt, and toss to coat. Arrange the broccoli florets evenly on the baking sheet, nestling them among the chickpeas.

Place the panko in the empty bowl and toss with the olive oil.

Sprinkle the Parmesan evenly over the baking sheet, topping the broccoli and chickpeas and filling in the empty areas among them. Sprinkle the panko evenly on top. Roast for 25 to 30 minutes, or until the broccoli is browned and the Parmesan and panko are golden brown and crisp.

Meanwhile, make the caper Caesar-ish dressing: In a medium bowl, stir together the mayonnaise, tahini, lemon juice, caper brine, capers, mustard, garlic, and several grinds of pepper. The dressing should have a creamy, drizzleable consistency. If it's too thick, add water, ½ teaspoon at a time, as needed to loosen it.

Remove the baking sheet from the oven and add the lettuce. Toss, then drizzle generously with the dressing. Serve immediately with the remaining dressing on the side.

SERVES **2** *TO* **4**

GLUTEN-FREE: Use gluten-free panko.

MORE WAYS TO USE

CAPERS

As a crispy topping.

Did you know you can fry capers? Blot them dry, then fry in olive oil over medium-high heat until crisp, just 1 to 2 minutes. Let drain on a paper towel–lined plate, then sprinkle over everything! I especially like them on blanched asparagus topped with creamy tarragon dill sauce (page 67).

On everything bagel dip.

Classic bagel fixings in dip form! Make the labneh on page 163. Spread it in a thin layer on a serving platter and top with capers, fresh dill, a drizzle of olive oil, and a big sprinkle of everything bagel seasoning. Serve with toasted mini bagels, bagel chips, and/or sliced cucumbers for dipping!

In a meal prep–able lentil salad

with shaved celery or fennel, parsley, red onion, and lemon vinaigrette (page 282).

In egg or potato salad.

A brinier alternative to chopped dill pickles.

In herby marinated white beans.

Fold white beans into the Italian salsa verde with capers on page 67. Add lemon zest and red pepper flakes and chill in the fridge to allow the flavors to meld. Enjoy on toast or in grain bowls, or make a bright bean salad by adding chopped avocado and cherry tomatoes.

In briny pasta puttanesca.

This classic Italian dish features a tomato sauce packed with capers and olives for tangy flavor. It would traditionally include anchovies too, but you can easily make a delicious veg version by adding extra capers. Top with parsley and basil!

On my favorite roasted cauliflower.

Roasted cauliflower florets + lemon vinaigrette (page 282) + olives + capers + parsley. Take it over the top with a sprinkle of lemon za'atar bread crumbs (page 130).

PICKLED SWEET CORN

My favorite summer vegetable? Corn, hands down. There's nothing like Midwest sweet corn, and when it comes into season, we eat it for months until we're completely corned out. If you love corn as much as I do, but you haven't thought of pickling it, put this recipe on your summer bucket list. It's the jumping-off point for some of my favorite recipes in the book, adding a quick hit of brightness to easy, breezy meals.

1 cup water, plus more as needed

⅓ cup distilled white vinegar

¼ cup fresh lime juice

2 tablespoons cane sugar

1½ teaspoons sea salt

Kernels from 3 ears corn (2¼ cups)

½ cup diced red onion

1 jalapeño pepper, stemmed and thinly sliced

1 garlic clove, halved

YIELD: ABOUT **3** *CUPS*

VEGAN | GLUTEN-FREE

Heat the water, vinegar, lime juice, sugar, and salt in a small saucepan over medium heat. Stir until the sugar and salt dissolve, about 1 minute. Remove from the heat and set aside to cool to room temperature.

In a medium bowl, toss together the corn, onion, and jalapeño. Evenly divide between two 16-ounce or similar-size lidded jars. Add ½ garlic clove to each jar.

Pour the cooled brine over the vegetables in the jars, pushing them down and adding more water as needed to fully submerge them. Cover and chill in the refrigerator overnight before using.

Store in the refrigerator for up to 2 weeks.

GRILLED ZUCCHINI WITH CREAMED CORN

& PICKLED SWEET CORN

The idea for this recipe came from a meal I had at the restaurant Modern Bird in Traverse City, Michigan. I ordered a dish that paired fresh creamed corn with a pickled corn topping, and I loved the exciting contrast of the two corn preparations. In developing my own version, I didn't make a true "creamed corn." Instead, blended corn gets mixed with polenta to create a creamy base for hearty grilled zucchini. Our pickled corn adds the perfect bright kick on top.

Creamed Corn Polenta

1 tablespoon extra-virgin olive oil

Kernels from 3 ears corn (2¼ cups)

3 garlic cloves, sliced

1 teaspoon sea salt

Freshly ground black pepper

⅛ teaspoon smoked paprika

3 cups water, plus more as needed

1 cup quick-cooking polenta

Grilled Zucchini

4 small zucchini (2 pounds), halved lengthwise

Extra-virgin olive oil, for drizzling

Sea salt and freshly ground black pepper

For Serving

½ cup crumbled cotija cheese

1⅔ cups Pickled Sweet Corn (page 250)

Fresh cilantro leaves

Make the creamed corn polenta: Heat the olive oil in a large skillet over medium heat. Add the corn kernels, garlic, ½ teaspoon of the salt, and several grinds of pepper. Cook, stirring, for 4 minutes, or until tender and bright yellow. Transfer to a blender and add the smoked paprika. Blend until smooth. If the mixture is too thick to blend, add water, 1 tablespoon at a time, as needed to create a smooth and creamy puree. Set aside while you cook the polenta.

Bring the water and the remaining ½ teaspoon salt to a boil in a medium pot. Gradually add the polenta, whisking continuously. Cook, whisking often, for 5 minutes, or until the polenta is tender, thick, and creamy. Reduce the heat to low as needed to prevent the polenta from sputtering as it thickens. The cooking times of different brands of polenta can vary. If your polenta is not tender after 5 minutes, add water as needed and continue cooking until tender, thick, and creamy.

Remove from the heat and stir in the corn puree and several grinds of pepper. Season to taste.

Make the grilled zucchini: Preheat a grill or grill pan to medium heat. Drizzle the zucchini with olive oil and sprinkle with salt and pepper. Grill cut side down for 3 minutes, or until char marks form. Flip and grill for 2 to 3 more minutes, or until tender and charred.

To serve, divide the polenta among four plates. Top each with two grilled zucchini halves, the cotija, and pickled sweet corn. Garnish with cilantro.

SERVES **4** | **VEGAN:** Skip the cheese or replace the cotija with vegan feta. | **GLUTEN-FREE**

TIP

Make these tacos a full meal for a group by serving them with black beans and a simple salad dressed with more of the pickled sweet corn brine.

CHILI LIME HALLOUMI TACOS

WITH PICKLED SWEET CORN

Summer might be the best season for produce, but it's also the season that I want to spend the least amount of time in the kitchen. When we have friends over, I want to be outside, sitting with a sparkling drink, not inside finishing dinner or shuffling too many things from the kitchen to the grill. Enter: these tacos. The pickled sweet corn in the filling does ALL the hard work. It's bright, perky, refreshing, and easy to make in advance. When you're ready to serve, just grill the halloumi and make a quick guacamole by mashing avocado with some of the pickled corn brine. Assemble the tacos with generous spoonfuls of the corn, and then leave the rest of the jar on the table in case anyone (raising my hand) wants more.

1 pound halloumi cheese, sliced into ½-inch-thick planks

Avocado oil, for drizzling

1 teaspoon chili powder

8 corn tortillas, warmed

Pickled Sweet Corn (page 250)

Fresh cilantro

Lime wedges, for serving

Quick Guacamole

2 avocados

1 tablespoon brine from Pickled Sweet Corn (page 250)

¼ teaspoon sea salt

Preheat a grill or grill pan to high heat.

Place the halloumi on a large plate. Drizzle with avocado oil, sprinkle with the chili powder, and rub both sides with your hands to coat.

Place the halloumi on the hot grill and reduce the heat to medium. Grill for 2 to 3 minutes per side, or until well charred.

Make the quick guacamole: In a medium bowl, mash the avocados with the pickled sweet corn brine and salt.

Assemble tacos in the tortillas with a scoop of the guacamole, the halloumi, a generous scoop of pickled sweet corn, and cilantro. Serve with lime wedges.

SERVES **4**

VEGAN: Replace the halloumi with high-protein tofu. Sprinkle with salt in addition to the chili powder before grilling.

GLUTEN-FREE: Use gluten-free corn tortillas.

CHILLED CUCUMBER SOUP

WITH PICKLED SWEET CORN

When I first moved to Austin, gazpacho quickly became one of my main food groups. When you live somewhere as hot as the surface of the sun, it's the ultimate way to cool down. I'd eat it as a pick-me-up after a sweaty run or serve it as a starter for a casual dinner party. Either way, I preferred it creamy, tangy, and topped with fun garnishes—which is where our pickled sweet corn comes in! It elevates this simple chilled soup with texture, spice, and bright flavor.

2 large English cucumbers (1¾ pounds)

3 small Green Zebra or yellow tomatoes (12 ounces), chopped

1½ cups blanched slivered almonds

¾ cup fresh cilantro, plus more for garnish

3 garlic cloves

¾ cup extra-virgin olive oil, plus more for drizzling

3 tablespoons white wine vinegar

1½ teaspoons sea salt

Freshly ground black pepper

1½ cups Pickled Sweet Corn (page 250), plus 6 tablespoons brine

Slice one of the cucumbers in half. Dice one of the halves and reserve for garnish.

Peel and chop the remaining 1½ cucumbers. Place in a high-speed blender and add the tomatoes, almonds, cilantro, garlic, olive oil, vinegar, salt, several grinds of pepper, and the 6 tablespoons pickled sweet corn brine. Blend until completely smooth and creamy, then chill in the refrigerator for at least 2 hours.

When ready to serve, stir the soup. It should have a creamy, pourable consistency. If it's too thick, stir in ¼ cup water, adding more, 2 tablespoons at a time, as needed to loosen it.

Pour into bowls and top with the reserved diced cucumber, pickled sweet corn, and cilantro. Drizzle with olive oil and serve.

SERVES **6**

VEGAN | GLUTEN-FREE

MORE WAYS TO USE

PICKLED SWEET CORN

On loaded guacamole.

The ultimate summer party dip!

In a summery avocado, cucumber, and mango salad.

Dress chopped avocado, cucumber, and mango in olive oil and a splash of pickled sweet corn brine. Gently mix with a scoop of the pickled corn and a handful of fresh mint.

In cheesy quesadillas

with black beans and/or your favorite veggies. Try it in the sheet pan quesadillas on page 75!

In a pickled sweet corn panzanella

with cubed stale bread, halved cherry tomatoes, sliced peaches, fresh mozzarella, and basil. Add plenty of olive oil and pickled sweet corn brine—the bread will soak it up and become insanely flavorful!

In a Southwest quinoa and black bean salad

with radishes, cilantro, and feta. Dress in olive oil and pickled sweet corn brine!

On creamy from-scratch beans,

like the pinto beans on page 177.

In stuffed poblano peppers.

Mix together a scoop of pickled corn, black beans, chopped avocado, and diced cherry tomatoes. Stuff into baked or grilled pepper halves and top with cilantro and cotija.

On tortilla soup or chili

for extra tang and crunch.

SLOW-ROASTED TOMATOES

Slow-roasted tomatoes are not a new concept, but they're something I lean on again and again when I want to make any dish pop with bright yet deep, tangy flavor. In fact, anytime I'm bringing a salad or a summery dish to a gathering, I almost always throw on slow-roasted tomatoes. I've found that even people who don't like tomatoes *love* these. They instantly elevate any bean or grain, and if you're looking for a truly showstopping party trick, make Phoebe's focaccia on page 265.

1 pint cherry tomatoes, halved

Extra-virgin olive oil, for drizzling

Sea salt and freshly ground black pepper

*YIELD: ABOUT **3/4** CUP*

VEGAN | GLUTEN-FREE

Preheat the oven to 250°F and line a baking sheet with parchment paper.

Spread the tomatoes evenly on the baking sheet, placing them cut side up. Drizzle with olive oil and sprinkle with salt and pepper.

Bake for 2 to 3 hours, or until the tomatoes are well shriveled around the edges. The exact timing will depend on the size and water content of your tomatoes.

Store in an airtight container in the refrigerator for up to 4 days or freeze for up to 3 months.

STUFFED EGGPLANT WITH FETA & MINT

& SLOW-ROASTED TOMATOES

I love stuffed eggplant in the summer—I've just never loved *making* it because I always felt like I had to add a lot of ingredients to develop a flavorful filling. I'd get carried away with nuts, dried fruit, grains, legumes, herbs, more herbs, and, and, and. But this recipe has less "ands" and simply relies on the amazing flavor of sweet, tangy roasted tomatoes. They're mixed into a lemon za'atar wheat berry salad to create a delightful fresh filling.

2 small-medium eggplants (about 1 pound)

Freshly ground black pepper

2 tablespoons extra-virgin olive oil, plus more for drizzling

Zest of 1 lemon

2 tablespoons fresh lemon juice

1 garlic clove, grated

½ teaspoon honey or maple syrup

½ teaspoon sea salt, plus more for sprinkling

½ teaspoon za'atar

3 cups cooked wheat berries or farro (page 320)

1 recipe Slow-Roasted Tomatoes (page 260)

½ cup roughly crumbled feta cheese

¼ cup fresh mint leaves

Red pepper flakes

Preheat the oven to 400°F and line a baking sheet with parchment paper.

Slice the eggplants in half lengthwise and scoop out the flesh, leaving a ½-inch rim around the edges. Drizzle the eggplant shells with olive oil, sprinkle with salt and pepper, and rub with your hands to coat. Place cut side down on the baking sheet and roast for 20 to 35 minutes, or until tender.

In a large bowl, whisk together the olive oil, lemon zest and juice, garlic, honey, salt, za'atar, and several grinds of pepper. Add the wheat berries and toss to coat. Gently fold in the roasted tomatoes and half the feta. Season to taste.

Spoon the wheat berry mixture into the eggplant halves and top with the remaining feta and mint. Sprinkle with red pepper flakes and serve.

SERVES **4**

VEGAN: Skip the feta or use vegan feta.

GLUTEN-FREE: Use quinoa or brown rice instead of wheat berries or farro.

FOCACCIA WITH SEA SALT & OLIVES

& SLOW-ROASTED TOMATOES

There's nothing more impressive than homemade focaccia! It's wonderful with just a sprinkle of sea salt, but to make it even better, add tangy slow-roasted tomatoes, briny olives, and a dash of herbes de Provence. I like to make this for Sunday dinners with my whole family. I always serve it with a simple pasta because I know the focaccia will be the star of the show.

1¾ cups warm water (105°F to 115°F)

2 teaspoons cane sugar

1 (¼-ounce) package active dry yeast (2¼ teaspoons)

4 cups all-purpose flour, spooned and leveled (see page 267)

2 teaspoons herbes de Provence

2 teaspoons sea salt

6 tablespoons extra-virgin olive oil, plus more for your hands and for brushing

1 recipe Slow-Roasted Tomatoes (page 260)

⅓ cup mixed olives, pitted and halved

Flaky sea salt

In the bowl of a stand mixer fitted with the dough hook, stir together the water and sugar. Sprinkle the yeast on top and stir again. Set aside for 5 minutes, or until the yeast is foamy. If the yeast doesn't foam, discard the mixture and start again with new yeast.

Add the flour, herbes de Provence, and salt and mix on low speed until a shaggy dough forms. Increase the speed to medium and mix for 5 minutes. A very elastic, sticky dough should form and begin grabbing the sides of the bowl.

Brush a large bowl with 2 tablespoons of the olive oil. Transfer the dough to the bowl, using a spatula to scrape it out of the bowl of the stand mixer. It will be too sticky to transfer by hand. Use your fingers to lightly brush any oil that's pooling at the edges of the dough over its surface. Cover the bowl with plastic wrap or a damp towel and set aside for 1 to 1½ hours, or until the dough has doubled in size.

Brush a 9×13-inch baking dish or quarter sheet pan with another 2 tablespoons of the olive oil. Uncover the dough and rub your

RECIPE CONTINUES

hands with olive oil. As best you can, slide your hand under one edge of the dough and fold it into itself. Continue working your way around the edge of the bowl, folding the dough into itself, until you have a rough ball that you can lift from the bowl.

Transfer the dough to the prepared pan and turn to coat in the oil. Press the dough to the pan's edges. Let it relax and pull away from the edges, then press it to the edges again. Cover the pan with plastic wrap or a damp towel and set aside to rise for 45 minutes, or until the dough has doubled in size. 30 minutes into this rise, preheat the oven to 400°F.

Remove the plastic wrap and drizzle the remaining 2 tablespoons olive oil over the dough. Rub your hands with olive oil, then use your fingers to make indentations across the surface of the dough, pressing through to the pan. Press the roasted tomatoes and olives into the top of the focaccia, arranging them evenly over the surface. Brush the toppings with a little more olive oil and sprinkle with flaky sea salt. Bake for 20 to 30 minutes, or until golden brown. If the toppings are getting too dark before the focaccia is ready, loosely cover the pan with foil and continue to bake until puffed and golden brown.

SERVES **8** *TO* **12**

VEGAN

HOW TO MEASURE FLOUR

Every time I call for flour in a recipe, I write "spooned and leveled" after it. Maybe you've noticed?

That's because flour can become compacted in a canister or measuring cup. It's easy to think you're adding the right amount to a recipe and actually use too much. Too much flour = dry baked goods. No thanks!

To accurately measure flour with a measuring cup, use the spoon-and-level method:

- Use a spoon to fluff up flour in its canister or bag.
- Gently spoon it into your measuring cup. Be careful not to pack it down—it should form a small mound above the rim.
- Clear off the excess flour by gently leveling the top with a knife.

Whatever you do, don't scoop up flour directly with your measuring cup—I can guarantee you'll use too much!

If you have a kitchen scale, another great option is to **weigh your flour**. For our recipes, 1 cup of flour is equivalent to 125 grams or 4.4 ounces.

CHARRED FENNEL WITH LEMONY BEANS

& SLOW-ROASTED TOMATOES

Vegetable trends come and go. When I first started blogging, cauliflower was all the rage. Then came kale—until everyone stopped eating kale (except me and Phoebe). All the while, I've been telling everyone I know that fennel is due for its day. It's so delicious and versatile! In this book, it's pickled, slaw-ed, Parmesan-ed, and, finally, charred as a knife-and-fork main dish. Zesty white beans make this a complete meal, and tangy roasted tomatoes take it over the top.

4 medium or 3 large fennel bulbs, trimmed

Extra-virgin olive oil, for drizzling

Sea salt and freshly ground black pepper

1 recipe Slow-Roasted Tomatoes (page 260)

¼ cup toasted pine nuts

Lemon wedges, for squeezing and serving (optional)

Fresh basil leaves, for garnish

For the Lemony Beans

2 tablespoons extra-virgin olive oil

1 tablespoon fresh lemon juice

1 teaspoon lemon zest

1 garlic clove, grated

¼ teaspoon red pepper flakes

¼ teaspoon sea salt

1½ cups cooked navy beans, drained and rinsed (page 320)

¼ cup chopped fresh parsley

Cut the fennel bulbs in half lengthwise. Bring a large pot of water to a boil. Add the fennel and boil for 12 minutes, or until starting to soften. Gently pat dry and set aside to drain.

Preheat the broiler and line a baking sheet with foil.

If your fennel bulbs are large, cut the halves in half lengthwise. Place the fennel on the baking sheet. Drizzle generously with olive oil and sprinkle with salt and pepper. Spread evenly on the baking sheet and broil for 20 to 25 minutes, or until tender and charred. Every broiler is different, so check the fennel often. Rotate the pan periodically and change racks as needed.

Meanwhile, make the lemony beans: In a large bowl, whisk together the olive oil, lemon juice and zest, garlic, red pepper flakes, and salt. Add the beans and parsley and gently stir to combine. Season to taste.

Remove the fennel from the oven and divide among four plates. Top with the beans, roasted tomatoes, and pine nuts. Squeeze lemon juice on top, if desired, and season with salt and pepper. Garnish with basil and serve with lemon wedges, if desired.

SERVES **4** | VEGAN | GLUTEN-FREE

MORE WAYS TO USE

SLOW-ROASTED TOMATOES

On cute crostini.

Spread crisp baguette slices with soft goat cheese and top with roasted tomatoes, toasted walnuts, and fresh thyme leaves. Drizzle with honey.

On creamy polenta.

Top a bowl of creamy polenta (or the creamed corn polenta on page 253) with a poached egg (page 81), roasted tomatoes, and basil pesto (page 66).

In a Caprese grilled cheese sandwich

with fresh mozzarella and basil.

In a grilled corn salad

with feta or fresh mozzarella, lemon vinaigrette (page 282), and any soft, leafy herbs. I often make this one a meal by adding cooked farro (page 320) too.

In a ratatouille-inspired frittata

with roasted or sautéed eggplant, zucchini, peppers, and basil or oregano.

In red pesto pasta.

Substitute 1 recipe slow-roasted tomatoes for the basil in the basil pesto on page 66. Toss with your favorite pasta, adding pasta water as needed to loosen the pesto into a lightly creamy sauce. Top with basil and Parm!

On pizza.

I especially love slow-roasted tomatoes on a white pizza. For a perfect summer pie, use them instead of the Fresno chiles on the ricotta arugula pizza on page 29. Skip the red pepper tahini and top the pizza with dollops of pesto (page 66) after baking instead.

KIMCHI

I first started loving fermented foods for their health benefits, but I've kept loving them for the bright, tangy flavor they bring to so many dishes. I almost always have a jar of kimchi, or Korean fermented vegetables, on hand to liven up any rice or noodle dish. Spoiler alert: It's also amazing blended into a sauce featured in two recipes in this chapter—two of my top favorites in the book. Store-bought kimchi can vary widely in quality; our favorite is Mother-in-Law's because it's easy to find in grocery stores and has a bolder, tangy flavor than other brands we've tried. Also note that traditional kimchi often contains fish sauce and/or shrimp paste. If you're vegan or vegetarian, make sure to buy a jar that's specifically labeled vegan.

BRUSSELS SPROUT TACOS

WITH KIMCHI & CREAMY KIMCHI SAUCE

These tacos are incredibly crave-worthy. They start with roasted Brussels sprouts and crispy baked tofu. While those are in the oven, more sprouts are shredded and tossed into a fresh slaw with kimchi, mint, and cilantro. Then there's a tangy, creamy kimchi sauce that gets drizzled on top. This sauce is a keeper—you'll love having it on hand for other uses too, like the gooey grilled cheese sandwiches on the next page!

Creamy Kimchi Sauce

½ cup kimchi with juices

⅓ cup mayonnaise

2 tablespoons water

1½ tablespoons avocado oil

1½ tablespoons toasted sesame oil

1½ teaspoons honey

1½ teaspoons sriracha

For the Tacos

1 pound Brussels sprouts

10 ounces high-protein tofu, patted dry and torn into big crumbles

Avocado oil, for drizzling

Tamari, for drizzling

½ cup chopped fresh cilantro, plus more cilantro leaves for garnish

¼ cup chopped fresh mint leaves

¼ cup thinly sliced kimchi

½ jalapeño pepper, stemmed and thinly sliced

1 tablespoon fresh lime juice

1 tablespoon toasted sesame oil

¼ teaspoon sea salt, plus more for sprinkling

8 tortillas, warmed

½ cup french-fried onions

Make the creamy kimchi sauce: In a blender, place the kimchi, mayonnaise, water, avocado oil, sesame oil, honey, and sriracha. Blend until smooth.

Make the tacos: Preheat the oven to 450°F and line a large baking sheet with parchment paper.

Trim and halve three-quarters of the Brussels sprouts and shred the remaining one-quarter. Set the shredded Brussels sprouts aside.

Place the halved Brussels sprouts on one side of the baking sheet and the tofu on the other side. Drizzle both with avocado oil. Sprinkle the Brussels sprouts with salt and drizzle the tofu with tamari. Toss to coat and spread evenly on the baking sheet. Bake for 22 to 27 minutes, or until the Brussels sprouts are browned and the tofu is crisp and browned.

Make the slaw. In a medium bowl, toss together the reserved shredded Brussels sprouts, cilantro, mint, kimchi, jalapeño, lime juice, sesame oil, and salt. Season to taste.

Assemble tacos in the tortillas with a spoonful of the kimchi sauce, the roasted Brussels sprouts and tofu, a scoop of the slaw, and more sauce. Sprinkle with the french-fried onions, garnish with cilantro, and serve.

SERVES **4**

VEGAN: Use vegan kimchi and vegan mayo. Use maple syrup instead of honey.

GLUTEN-FREE: Use certified gluten-free tamari and gluten-free tortillas. Skip the fried onions or use gluten-free fried onions.

KIMCHI GRILLED CHEESE

WITH CREAMY KIMCHI SAUCE

Oh hi, welcome to the next page. If you made the creamy kimchi sauce from the Brussels sprout taco recipe on page 275, here's the easiest—and most fun (!)—way to use up the rest of that sauce. If you didn't come from that page, make this recipe first, then go try those tacos. They're two of my favorite recipes in the book, thanks to that tangy kimchi sauce—it's just so . . . darn . . . good. In fact, the first time I used it on a grilled cheese sandwich for lunch, I was so excited about it that I made another one the very next day.

8 slices sourdough or country bread
Mayonnaise, for the bread
8 ounces grated white cheddar cheese
¼ cup Creamy Kimchi Sauce (page 275)
1 cup kimchi, roughly chopped
4 scallions, chopped
¼ cup chopped fresh cilantro
Avocado oil, for the pan

Place the bread slices on a cutting board and spread the top side with a thin layer of mayonnaise. Flip four of the slices and evenly divide half the cheddar among them. Drizzle with the kimchi sauce, then top with the kimchi, scallions, cilantro, and remaining cheese. Place the remaining four bread slices on top of the cheese, mayo side out.

Heat a nonstick or cast-iron skillet over medium-low heat and lightly coat the bottom with avocado oil. Working in batches if necessary, place the sandwiches in the pan, cover, and cook for 2 to 3 minutes, or until the bottom bread slices are golden brown and crisp. Flip, then use a spatula to lightly push down on the top of each sandwich. Replace the lid and cook for 2 to 4 more minutes, or until the sandwiches are golden brown on both sides and the cheese is melted. Reduce the heat to low if the bread is getting too brown before the cheese is fully melted.

Slice in half and serve.

SERVES **4**

GLUTEN-FREE: Use gluten-free bread.

TIP

Spice up this soup by topping your bowl with a scoop of chili crisp!

SHIITAKE VEGGIE NOODLE SOUP

WITH KIMCHI

This is the ultimate feel-good soup. The simple broth comes together with shiitake mushrooms, scallions, and tamari, plus kimchi and rice vinegar for tang. It's filled with half noodles and half strips of vegetables that act like noodles, so you get it all in one slurp. It's nourishing and comforting, and surprisingly, even our four-year-old loves it, so it's become a family favorite.

2 tablespoons avocado oil

8 ounces shiitake mushrooms, stemmed and sliced

1 bunch scallions, chopped

1 cup chopped kimchi

2 teaspoons grated fresh ginger

4 cups vegetable broth

2 cups water

2½ tablespoons tamari, plus more for serving

2 tablespoons rice vinegar

4 ounces soba noodles, cooked

1 medium zucchini, julienned*

1 large carrot, julienned*

Soft-boiled eggs, for serving (page 321, optional)

Sesame seeds, for garnish

Sriracha, for serving (optional)

** I have a small handheld julienne peeler that makes the vegetables easy to cut.*

Heat the avocado oil in a large pot or Dutch oven over medium heat. Add the mushrooms and cook, stirring occasionally, for 5 to 8 minutes, or until soft and browned. Add most of the scallions, reserving some for garnish, then add the kimchi and ginger and cook for 30 seconds, or until fragrant. Add the broth, water, tamari, and rice vinegar and simmer, uncovered, for 15 minutes.

Add the soba noodles, zucchini, and carrot and cook for 5 minutes, or until softened. Season to taste.

Portion into bowls and top with soft-boiled eggs, if desired. Garnish with sesame seeds and the reserved scallions. Serve with more tamari and sriracha on the side, if desired.

SERVES **4**

VEGAN: Use vegan kimchi and skip the eggs.

GLUTEN-FREE: Use certified gluten-free tamari and 100 percent buckwheat soba noodles.

MORE WAYS TO USE

KIMCHI

In a crunchy cucumber salad.

Toss chopped cucumbers with chopped kimchi and drizzles of tamari and toasted sesame oil. Serve topped with cilantro and sprinkles of sesame nori crisp (page 140).

In savory, garlicky noodles.

Toss cooked rice or wheat noodles with a light dressing made from rice vinegar, tamari, grated garlic, and toasted sesame oil. Top with kimchi, scallions, and sautéed shiitake mushrooms.

In extra-veggie fried rice.

A perfect use for leftover rice and whatever veggies you need to use up! Chopped napa cabbage, snow peas, carrots, shiitake mushrooms, scallions, white onion, and corn are some of my favorites to use here. The kimchi makes the whole thing pop!

In creamy tofu "egg salad."

Fold diced extra-firm tofu into mayo or vegan mayo with a squirt of sriracha, chopped kimchi, scallions, cilantro, and sesame seeds. Enjoy as you would egg salad—on a sandwich, in a wrap, with crackers, or over greens.

On crispy rice bowls.

I love making the crispy rice bowls on page 85 with kimchi instead of chili crisp! A bibimbap-inspired bowl with a fried egg and sautéed veggies like mushrooms, spinach, and/or mung bean sprouts is great too. Top with kimchi and serve with gochujang on the side.

5 ESSENTIAL LEMON RECIPES

By now, you get it—I love lemons. So I thought it would be fitting to end this Tangy chapter with a few of my go-to little lemon recipes. Keep any of these on hand to add a citrusy pop of flavor to whatever you're cooking!

1

LEMON VINAIGRETTE

¼ cup olive oil
¼ cup lemon juice
1 garlic clove, grated
1 teaspoon Dijon mustard
½ teaspoon sea salt
¼ teaspoon dried thyme
Freshly ground black pepper

Whisk together.

2

LEMON HARISSA OIL

⅓ cup olive oil
¼ teaspoon whole caraway seeds, crushed
¼ teaspoon whole coriander seeds, crushed
¼ teaspoon whole cumin seeds, crushed
1 teaspoon lemon zest
1 tablespoon spicy harissa

Heat the oil in a small skillet over medium heat. Add the spices and cook for 15 seconds to 1 minute, or until fragrant. Transfer to a heatproof bowl. Stir in the lemon zest and harissa. Drizzle over grilled or roasted vegetables, creamy dips, and soups.

3

LEMON TONIC

1½ cups water
1 (2-inch) piece fresh ginger, thinly sliced
6 individual fresh thyme sticks
¼ cup lemon juice
1 tablespoon honey

In a small saucepan, simmer the water, ginger, and thyme for 5 minutes. Remove from the heat, cover, and steep for 10 minutes.

Remove the ginger and thyme, then stir in the lemon juice and honey. Sip warm or chill to use in cocktails and mocktails.

4

LEMON FENNEL PICKLE

1 medium organic lemon, very thinly sliced on a mandoline and seeded (¾ cup)
1 small fennel bulb, very thinly sliced on a mandoline (¾ cup)
1 Fresno chile, stemmed and thinly sliced
¼ cup lemon juice
1½ teaspoons sugar
½ teaspoon sea salt
2 tablespoons water, plus more as needed

Halve the lemon slices to form half-moons, removing any coarse white pith from the center of the slices.

Place the lemons, fennel, chile, lemon juice, sugar, and salt in a lidded jar. Cover and shake to combine.

Remove the lid and push the mixture into an even layer. Add the water, adding more as needed to cover. Chill overnight before using on salads, pastas, sandwiches, and toasts.

5

ROASTED LEMON MARMALADE

4 organic lemons
Olive oil, for drizzling
Sea salt
3 tablespoons honey
Pinch of red pepper flakes

Preheat the oven to 350°F and line two baking sheets with parchment paper.

Cut off and discard the ends of the lemons, then cut the lemons into ¼-inch-thick slices. Remove the seeds.

Arrange the slices evenly on the baking sheets. Drizzle with oil and sprinkle both sides with salt. Roast for 20 minutes, then flip. Roast for 15 to 20 minutes, or until lightly caramelized.

Remove from the oven and dice. Transfer to a bowl and mix with the honey and red pepper flakes. Slather on toast or serve on a cheese board.

SPAGHETTI AGLIO E OLIO

WITH LEMON FENNEL PICKLE

Spaghetti aglio e olio is my go-to back-pocket pasta. Whenever it feels like there's nothing in the fridge except a bunch of parsley, this is what I make. I love it because it's super simple and easily riffable—though I'm pretty sure my Italian ancestors wouldn't approve of how often I mess with the classic. But honestly, that's just because they haven't tried *this* version with lemon fennel pickles. The lemon adds a tangy pop, the fennel gives it some crunch, and Fresno chiles bring the heat. A little surprise herb—tarragon—makes it extra-fresh and herby too.

12 ounces spaghetti pasta

¼ cup extra-virgin olive oil

5 garlic cloves, thinly sliced

¼ teaspoon red pepper flakes

½ teaspoon sea salt

1½ cups fresh parsley leaves, finely chopped (from about 1 large bunch)

¼ cup fresh tarragon leaves, finely chopped

½ cup Lemon Fennel Pickle (page 283), plus more for serving

Fresh basil leaves, for garnish

Bring a large pot of salted water to a boil. Prepare the pasta according to the package instructions, cooking until al dente.

A few minutes before the pasta is ready, heat the olive oil in a large skillet over medium-low heat. Add the garlic and red pepper flakes and cook, stirring, for 2 to 3 minutes, or until the garlic is fragrant and just beginning to turn golden brown. Remove from the heat.

When the pasta is al dente, use tongs to transfer it from the pot to the skillet with the garlic and oil. Toss to coat in the oil, then add the salt, parsley, and tarragon and toss again. If the pasta seems dry, add pasta water, ¼ cup at a time, as needed to create a light sauce.

Add the lemon fennel pickle and toss to combine. Season to taste, garnish with basil, and serve with more lemon fennel pickle as desired.

SERVES **4**

VEGAN

GLUTEN-FREE: Use gluten-free spaghetti.

HONEY RICOTTA TOAST

WITH ROASTED LEMON MARMALADE

This recipe wins the Love & Lemons award for being the most lemony one in the book! This marmalade uses the whole lemon—rind and all. Lemon slices become sweet and almost jammy when roasted, so we thought, why not make jam? Creamy ricotta and a drizzle of honey perfectly balance the tartness of the marmalade. Note: If you can find Meyer lemons, their tender skins and subtle sweetness add a special touch to this recipe.

2 slices crusty sourdough bread, toasted

Whole milk ricotta cheese

Roasted Lemon Marmalade (page 283)

Extra-virgin olive oil, for drizzling

Honey, for drizzling

Fresh thyme leaves, for garnish

Slather the toast with ricotta and spoon roasted lemon marmalade on top. Drizzle with olive oil and honey.

Garnish with thyme and serve.

SERVES **2** *TO* **4**

GLUTEN-FREE: Use gluten-free bread.

LEMON GINGER THYME COCKTAIL

WITH LEMON TONIC

Here's my unpopular opinion: I think all cocktails should have herbs. The best cocktail I've ever had was a gin drink mixed with Thai basil. Another favorite is a mezcal cocktail garnished with smoking rosemary. And then, of course, there's my own cocktail with blueberry mint shrub on page 213. What I hadn't tried until now was a thyme cocktail—so it was about thyme! (Sorry, not sorry.) This zesty, bright, and earthy drink is absolutely delicious.

2 ounces ginger kombucha
2 ounces Lemon Tonic (page 283)
1 ounce gin
Ice
Fresh thyme sprig, for garnish
Lemon slice, for garnish

Add the kombucha, lemon tonic, gin, and a few ice cubes to a mixing glass. Stir until chilled.

Strain into a chilled coupe glass. Garnish with the thyme and lemon slice and serve.

SERVES **1**

VEGAN: Make the lemon tonic with maple syrup instead of honey.

GLUTEN-FREE

CHAPTER 6

SWEET

Who else is ready for dessert?! In the spirit of indulgence, we're breaking the rules a little in this chapter. Instead of organizing it by components, I've included some of my favorite saucy, spicy, crunchy, herby, and tangy treats. If you ask me, the most craveable desserts are never *just* sweet.

TIP

This cherry sauce is also delicious on ice cream, pancakes, or anything that needs a fruity pop!

ALMOND CAKE

WITH CHERRY POMEGRANATE SAUCE

After spending so much time in Northern Michigan, my co-author Phoebe and I have developed a serious love of cherries, and we wanted to create a dessert that would really celebrate them. This easy, stir-together almond cake is the perfect base for an incredible cherry sauce that we're totally obsessed with. It's sweet and jammy, and thanks to a secret ingredient—pomegranate molasses—it has this amazing tangy pop. The best part? If you don't have fresh, in-season cherries, the sauce is just as good with frozen ones from the supermarket.

Cherry Pomegranate Sauce

2 pounds pitted cherries, thawed if frozen

¼ cup cane sugar

2 tablespoons pomegranate molasses

Pinch of sea salt

Almond Cake

1½ cups all-purpose flour, spooned and leveled (see page 267)

¾ cup almond flour, spooned and leveled (see page 267)

1 tablespoon baking powder

1 teaspoon cinnamon

1 teaspoon sea salt

1¼ cups whole milk Greek yogurt

¾ cup cane sugar

¾ cup extra-virgin olive oil, plus more for the pan

3 large eggs

½ teaspoon almond extract

Whole milk Greek yogurt or whipped cream, for serving

Make the cherry pomegranate sauce: Measure 1 cup of the cherries and set aside.

In a large skillet, combine the remaining cherries, sugar, pomegranate molasses, and salt. Cook, stirring, over medium heat for 1 minute, or until the sugar dissolves, then simmer, stirring occasionally, for 20 minutes. Add the reserved 1 cup cherries and continue to cook, stirring occasionally, for another 10 minutes to reduce the cherry juices slightly. Set aside to cool to room temperature, then transfer to an airtight container and chill in the refrigerator until ready to serve.

Make the almond cake: Preheat the oven to 350°F and grease a 9-inch round cake pan. Line the bottom with parchment paper.

In a medium bowl, whisk together the all-purpose and almond flours, baking powder, cinnamon, and salt.

In a large bowl, whisk together the yogurt, sugar, olive oil, eggs, and almond extract. Add the dry ingredients to the wet ingredients and mix until just combined.

Transfer the batter to the prepared pan and smooth the top. Bake for 35 to 40 minutes, or until a toothpick inserted comes out clean. Allow to cool in the pan for 15 minutes before turning out and transferring to a wire rack to cool completely.

Slice and serve topped with a dollop of yogurt or whipped cream and the cherry pomegranate sauce.

SERVES **8** *TO* **12**

TIP

Try another sauce! The miso peanut caramel sauce isn't the only one that's great on these brownies. We love them with Chocolate Tahini Sauce (page 317) and Strawberry Balsamic Sauce (page 319) too.

ONE-BOWL BANANA BROWNIES

WITH MISO PEANUT CARAMEL SAUCE

This caramel sauce is one to hide in the back of the fridge so that no one else finds it—it just disappears too fast. Luckily, it couldn't be easier to make. It takes literally a minute to stir together on the stove! It's the perfect match for these decadent banana brownies. They're moist, gooey, and full of chocolatey banana flavor. Just a heads-up: You'll want to take them out of the oven when they still seem the tiniest bit underdone. They'll set up with a delicious fudgy texture and be easy to slice once they've cooled—if you can wait that long to try them.

½ cup mashed very ripe banana (about 1 large)

¾ cup granulated sugar

½ cup powdered sugar, sifted if lumpy

½ cup vegetable oil or other neutral oil, plus more for the pan

1 large egg

½ teaspoon vanilla extract

⅔ cup unsweetened cocoa powder, sifted if lumpy

½ teaspoon sea salt

⅔ cup all-purpose flour, spooned and leveled (see page 267)

½ cup chopped dark chocolate

½ cup chopped walnuts

Vanilla ice cream, for serving

Miso Peanut Caramel Sauce

½ cup creamy natural peanut butter

3 tablespoons maple syrup

1 tablespoon white miso paste

1 teaspoon vanilla extract

½ cup plus 2 tablespoons unsweetened almond milk, plus more as needed

Preheat the oven to 325°F and grease an 8×8-inch baking dish. Line the bottom and two of the sides with a sheet of parchment paper. Grease the parchment paper.

In a large bowl, whisk together the mashed banana, granulated and powdered sugars, vegetable oil, egg, and vanilla.

Sprinkle the cocoa powder and salt evenly over the mixture and mix until combined. Sprinkle the flour over the mixture and mix until mostly combined, then add the chopped chocolate and walnuts and mix until well combined.

Transfer the batter to the prepared pan and smooth the top. Bake for 32 to 42 minutes, or until the top is set and a toothpick inserted comes out mostly clean. Allow to cool completely in the pan.

Meanwhile, make the miso peanut caramel sauce: In a small saucepan, combine the peanut butter, maple syrup, miso, and vanilla. Cook, stirring, over low heat until the miso is incorporated. Gradually add the almond milk while whisking and continue to whisk for 1 minute, or until the sauce is smooth. Add more almond milk, 1 tablespoon at a time, as needed to reach a drizzleable consistency.

Slice and serve the brownies topped with vanilla ice cream and the miso peanut caramel sauce.

SERVES **16**

VEGAN: Omit the egg and increase the mashed banana to ¾ cup (about 1½ large). Use vegan chocolate. Increase the bake time to 40 to 50 minutes and serve with vegan ice cream.

**If you're not using a high-speed blender, soak the cashews for at least 4 hours or overnight before blending them. You may need to blend the cheesecake mixture longer to achieve a smooth and creamy texture.*

VEGAN CHEESECAKE PARFAITS

WITH SAUCY APPLES

My mom makes the best cheesecake. Before her, my grandma Kissel made the best cheesecake. It's a family recipe that's special because it's decadent yet somehow light, thanks to a top-secret ingredient ratio and a very particular baking technique. I'd tell you all about it—except my mom doesn't give out the recipe, even to me! Still, when I taste these parfaits, they bring back all of my cheesecake nostalgia. They're good with any fruit, but for a cozy fall twist, saucy apples send them straight over the top.

Graham Cracker Crust

8 vegan graham crackers (4 full cracker sheets, 4 ounces)

¼ cup packed brown sugar

¼ cup melted coconut oil

Heaping ¼ teaspoon sea salt

Creamy Cheesecake Filling

2 (8-ounce) packages vegan cream cheese, at room temperature

1 cup raw cashews*

⅔ cup powdered sugar

3 tablespoons fresh lemon juice

2 teaspoons vanilla extract

Saucy Apples

5 medium apples (about 2 pounds), peeled, cored, and thinly sliced

7 tablespoons water

1 tablespoon fresh lemon juice

1 teaspoon cinnamon

¼ teaspoon ground ginger

¼ teaspoon nutmeg

Pinch of sea salt

1 teaspoon cornstarch

Make the graham cracker crust: In a food processor, place the graham crackers, brown sugar, coconut oil, and salt and pulse until finely ground. Divide among six small jars. Press lightly into the bottoms.

Make the creamy cheesecake filling: In a high-speed blender, place the vegan cream cheese, cashews, powdered sugar, lemon juice, and vanilla. Blend until smooth and creamy. If the mixture is too thick to blend, add water, ¼ cup at a time, as needed to reach a smooth and creamy consistency. I find that some brands of vegan cream cheese blend well with no added water and others need ½ cup or slightly more. Evenly divide among the jars. Cover and chill in the refrigerator for at least 2 hours or overnight.

Make the saucy apples: In a large saucepan, combine the apples, 2 tablespoons of the water, the lemon juice, cinnamon, ginger, nutmeg, and salt. Cover and cook, stirring occasionally, over medium-low heat for 10 minutes. Add 4 more tablespoons of the water and continue to cook, covered, for another 5 minutes, or until the apples are tender and juicy.

In a small bowl, stir together the cornstarch and the remaining 1 tablespoon water. Add to the apples and cook for 1 minute, or until the juices bubble and thicken slightly. Allow to cool to room temperature, then chill until ready to serve.

Assemble the parfaits by dividing the apples and their juices among the jars.

SERVES **6** | **VEGAN** | **GLUTEN-FREE:** Use gluten-free graham crackers.

TIP

You might have a little of the chai tea mixture left over—save it and mix a few splashes with steamed milk for a bonus homemade chai latte.

COZY AUTUMN PUMPKIN LOAF

WITH CHAI SPICES

As summer comes to a close, everyone on social media goes crazy for pumpkin-spiced everything—a little too crazy, if you ask me. You won't see me baking pumpkin bread in August, but once there's actually a chill in the air, I'm ALL about this PSL-inspired loaf. It starts with a boldly concentrated chai tea mixture that gets baked into the bread and also stirred into the glaze. It's a serious upgrade to pumpkin bread, and it's one of my favorite sweet treats in this book!

3 star anise

1 teaspoon whole black peppercorns

1 cup unsweetened almond milk

1 (1-inch) piece fresh ginger, thinly sliced

1 black tea bag

2 cups all-purpose flour, spooned and leveled (see page 267)

2 teaspoons baking powder

2 teaspoons cinnamon

1 teaspoon ground cardamom

½ teaspoon baking soda

½ teaspoon sea salt

1 cup canned pumpkin puree

¾ cup packed brown sugar

½ cup vegetable oil or other neutral oil, plus more for the pan

2 large eggs

1 teaspoon vanilla extract

1 cup powdered sugar, sifted if lumpy

In a small saucepan, combine the star anise and black peppercorns. Toast over medium heat for 1 to 2 minutes, or until fragrant. Add the almond milk and ginger and reduce the heat to low. Gently simmer for 5 minutes. Remove from the heat and add the tea bag. Cover and steep for 10 minutes, then strain to remove the spices, tea bag, and ginger. Set aside to cool slightly.

Preheat the oven to 350°F and grease an 8×4-inch loaf pan. Line the bottom and two long sides with a sheet of parchment paper.

In a medium bowl, whisk together the flour, baking powder, cinnamon, cardamom, baking soda, and salt.

Measure ½ cup of the infused almond milk and place in a large bowl, reserving the remaining almond milk. To the large bowl, add the pumpkin puree, brown sugar, vegetable oil, eggs, and vanilla and whisk until combined. Add the dry ingredients to the wet ingredients and mix until just combined.

Transfer the batter to the prepared pan and smooth the top. Bake for 55 to 65 minutes, or until a toothpick inserted comes out clean. Allow to cool completely.

In a small bowl, whisk together the powdered sugar and 1½ tablespoons of the reserved infused almond milk to create a thick, smooth glaze. Pour over the cooled loaf. Set aside for 10 minutes for the glaze to set, then slice and serve.

SERVES **8**

VEGAN: Mix 2 tablespoons ground flaxseed with ⅓ cup water. Let thicken for 5 minutes, then add to the recipe in place of the eggs. Increase the baking powder to 1 tablespoon.

MEXICAN HOT CHOCOLATE FREEZER BARS

WITH CINNAMON & CAYENNE

Raise your hand if you love a spicy dessert! Okay, okay—maybe I'm one of the only ones with my hand up, but trust me: a little hint of cayenne paired with chocolate, a touch of orange, and coconut-vanilla goodness is *next-level* delicious.

1 (13.5-ounce) can coconut cream

2 cups raw cashews*

⅓ cup maple syrup

¼ cup fresh orange juice

¼ cup water

½ teaspoon vanilla extract

⅛ teaspoon sea salt

2 tablespoons unsweetened cocoa powder

¼ teaspoon cayenne pepper, plus a pinch for dusting

⅛ teaspoon cinnamon, plus ½ teaspoon for dusting

¼ cup dark chocolate chips

1 teaspoon coconut oil

**If you're not using a high-speed blender, soak the cashews for at least 4 hours or overnight before blending them. You may need to blend the cashew mixture longer to achieve a smooth texture.*

Line the bottom and two long sides of an 8×4-inch loaf pan with a sheet of parchment paper.

In a high-speed blender, place the coconut cream, cashews, maple syrup, orange juice, water, vanilla, and salt. Blend until smooth. Measure 1½ cups of the cashew mixture and set aside.

To the remaining mixture in the blender, add the cocoa powder, cayenne, and cinnamon. Blend until combined.

Pour the chocolate mixture into the prepared pan and smooth the top. Freeze for 1 hour, then pour on the reserved cashew mixture and smooth the top. Freeze for at least 3 hours.

In a small microwave-safe bowl, combine the chocolate chips and coconut oil. Microwave for 1 to 3 minutes, stirring every 20 seconds, or until melted and smooth.

Remove the pan from the freezer. Drizzle the bars with the melted chocolate. Combine the ½ teaspoon cinnamon and pinch of cayenne in a sifter and dust over the bars. Freeze for 10 minutes, or until the melted chocolate is firm.

Slice into bars. If the bars are too firm to slice, let them sit at room temperature for 10 minutes to soften before slicing and serving.

Store leftover bars in the freezer.

SERVES **12**

VEGAN: Use vegan chocolate chips.

GLUTEN-FREE

MISO CHOCOLATE CHIP COOKIES

WITH LOTS OF CRUNCHY THINGS

These are hands down my favorite chocolate chip cookies. I know cookie preference is a personal thing, but for me, these have everything. There's a nice balance of sweetness and rich saltiness (thank you, miso), they're chewy in the middle, and they're loaded with gooey chocolate. Since this recipe is a nod to the Crunchy chapter, we basically raided the pantry for all of our favorite crunchy things to give these cookies wonderful texture and nutty depth of flavor.

1 cup packed dark brown sugar

½ cup melted coconut oil

½ cup smooth almond butter

¼ cup water

¼ cup white miso paste

2 teaspoons vanilla extract

1 teaspoon baking powder

½ teaspoon baking soda

1½ cups all-purpose flour, spooned and leveled (see page 267)

½ cup chopped dark chocolate

½ cup chopped pecans or walnuts

½ cup chopped roasted unsalted peanuts

2 tablespoons pepitas

2 tablespoons sesame seeds

Preheat the oven to 350°F and line two baking sheets with parchment paper.

In a large bowl, whisk together the brown sugar, coconut oil, almond butter, water, miso, and vanilla until smooth. Sprinkle the baking powder and baking soda evenly over the mixture and whisk to combine.

Sprinkle the flour over the mixture and use a spatula to mix until partially combined, then add the chocolate, pecans, peanuts, pepitas, and sesame seeds and mix until well combined.

Use a 2-tablespoon cookie scoop to scoop the dough onto the baking sheets, leaving at least 2 inches between cookies. Bake, one sheet at a time, for 12 to 14 minutes, or until lightly browned around the edges. Let cool on the baking sheets for 10 minutes before transferring to a wire rack to cool completely.

MAKES ABOUT **25** *COOKIES*

VEGAN: Use vegan chocolate.

SUMMER STRAWBERRY BARS

WITH PRETZEL CRUMBLE

When I was growing up in the Midwest, one of my favorite summer desserts was strawberry pretzel salad. If you're not familiar with it . . . well, for starters, it's not a salad. It's a layered, Jell-O-based dessert with a crunchy pretzel crust. For our spin on this nostalgic recipe, we skipped the Jell-O and made bars instead! They're bursting with fresh strawberries and feature a buttery pretzel crust that also serves as the crumble topping.

4 cups salted pretzel twists (6 ounces)

1 cup all-purpose flour, spooned and leveled (see page 267)

1 cup packed light brown sugar

¼ teaspoon sea salt

12 tablespoons (1½ sticks) unsalted butter, melted, plus more for the pan

1 pound fresh strawberries, hulled and diced

2 tablespoons cane sugar

2 teaspoons cornstarch

Preheat the oven to 350°F and grease an 8×8-inch baking dish. Line the bottom and two of the sides with a sheet of parchment paper.

Place the pretzels in a food processor and pulse until about half are ground into a fine powder and half are left in larger chunks. Transfer to a large bowl and add the flour, brown sugar, and salt. Stir to combine, then drizzle in the butter. Use your hands to mix until all the dry ingredients are moistened and the mixture holds together when pinched.

Measure 1½ cups of the crumble and set aside for the topping. Transfer the remaining crumble to the prepared pan and use your hands or the bottom of a measuring cup to press it evenly across the bottom. Bake for 10 minutes, or until lightly set. Leave the oven on.

Meanwhile, prepare the filling. In a medium saucepan, combine the strawberries and sugar. Cook, stirring occasionally, over medium heat for 4 minutes, or until the strawberries release some of their juices and begin to break down. Stir in the cornstarch and cook for 1 minute, or until the strawberries bubble and thicken. Remove from the heat.

Spread the strawberries evenly over the par-baked crust. If the reserved pretzel crumble is dry, add water, ½ teaspoon at a time, as needed to help it clump up. Sprinkle the crumble evenly over the bars and bake for 22 to 27 minutes, or until the strawberries are bubbling and the topping is crisp.

Remove from the oven and allow to cool completely in the pan before slicing and serving.

SERVES **16**

VEGAN: Use vegan butter and omit the salt.

LEMON PISTACHIO COOKIES

WITH BASIL

You might not be surprised that one of my favorite flavor combinations is lemon and basil. They're two easy ingredients to use all summer long while my basil plant is thriving, but basil's natural sweetness lends itself not only to savory foods but to desserts too.

- 1 cup shelled raw pistachios, plus 2 tablespoons crushed pistachios for topping
- 1 cup cane sugar
- 2 tablespoons lemon zest
- ⅔ cup extra-virgin olive oil
- 1 large egg
- 1 large egg yolk
- 1 teaspoon vanilla extract
- ½ teaspoon baking powder
- ½ teaspoon sea salt
- ⅓ cup chopped fresh basil leaves
- 1½ cups all-purpose flour, spooned and leveled (see page 267)

Preheat the oven to 375°F and line two large baking sheets with parchment paper.

Place 1 cup of the pistachios in a food processor and pulse until most are finely ground but some larger pieces remain. Set aside.

In a large bowl, place the cane sugar and lemon zest. Use your fingers to work the zest into the sugar until well combined. This helps the zest release its fragrant oils. Add the olive oil and whisk until well combined, then add the egg, egg yolk, and vanilla and whisk until smooth.

Sprinkle the baking powder and salt evenly over the mixture, then whisk to combine. Use a spatula to mix in the basil.

Add the flour and mix until mostly combined, then add the ground pistachios and mix until well combined. Use a 2-tablespoon cookie scoop to scoop the dough onto the baking sheets, leaving at least 2 inches between cookies. Sprinkle the tops with the remaining 2 tablespoons crushed pistachios, pressing down lightly so that they stick to the cookies.

Bake, one sheet at a time, for 9 to 11 minutes, or until the cookies are lightly golden brown underneath and tiny cracks form in the tops. They will be lightly set around the edges but still look pale and underdone in the middle. That's okay—they will set up as they cool. Let cool on the baking sheets for 10 minutes before transferring to a wire rack to cool completely.

MAKES ABOUT **24** *COOKIES*

WATERMELON GRANITA

WITH MINTY SIMPLE SYRUP

When my sister and I were growing up, we used to set up lemonade stands with our neighborhood friends in the summer. At our best events, we also sold snow cones. We'd make them in our Snoopy Sno-Cone Machine, which was too difficult to crank without a parent's help. Luckily, someone would always oblige, and soon there'd be snow cones for all of us kids. We'd drizzle on the overly sticky syrups and forget we were supposed to be selling them in the first place.

Luckily, this recipe doesn't require a Snoopy Sno-Cone Machine or brightly colored fake syrups, but it's just as delightfully refreshing. Delicate icy shavings of lime-scented watermelon are drizzled with minty simple syrup for the ultimate treat on a hot afternoon.

4 cups cubed seedless watermelon (1½ pounds)

Zest of 1 lime

¼ cup fresh lime juice

2 tablespoons cane sugar

Pinch of sea salt

Fresh mint leaves, for garnish

Minty Simple Syrup

½ cup water

½ cup cane sugar

1 cup fresh mint leaves

In a blender, place the watermelon, lime zest and juice, sugar, and salt. Blend until smooth and pour into a 9×13-inch baking dish.

Freeze for 1 hour, then remove the watermelon mixture from the freezer. Scrape the tines of a fork through the mixture, shaving any ice crystals into small pieces. Repeat the freezing and shaving process twice, scraping through the mixture every hour, until all the granita is frozen and shaved.

Meanwhile, make the minty simple syrup: Heat the water and sugar in a small saucepan over medium heat. Cook, stirring occasionally, for 2 minutes, or until the sugar dissolves. Remove from the heat and add the mint leaves. Cover and steep for 20 minutes, then strain to remove the mint. Chill in the refrigerator until ready to serve.

Portion the granita into serving bowls and drizzle with a little of the minty simple syrup. Garnish with mint and serve.

SERVES **6**

VEGAN | GLUTEN-FREE

CARROT SNACK CAKE

WITH TANGY TAHINI FROSTING

I couldn't write a book without including some type of carrot cake recipe. Carrot cake is a family favorite (my mom makes one every year for Jack's birthday) and a reader favorite (the Carrot Cake Bars in *Simple Feel Good Food* went viral before the book even came out). So how to top that? Three words: tangy tahini frosting. Adding tahini and lemon juice to classic cream cheese frosting gives it a brighter kick and a rich, nutty flavor. Try not to eat it all straight out of the mixing bowl before it makes it onto the cake.

1¼ cups all-purpose flour, spooned and leveled (see page 267)

½ cup whole wheat flour, spooned and leveled (see page 267)

1½ teaspoons baking powder

1½ teaspoons cinnamon

1 teaspoon ground ginger

¾ teaspoon sea salt

½ teaspoon baking soda

½ teaspoon ground cardamom

¾ cup packed brown sugar

3 large eggs

½ cup unsweetened applesauce

½ cup vegetable oil or other neutral oil, plus more for the pan

1½ teaspoons vanilla extract

2 cups finely grated carrots (7 ounces, about 3 large)

4 soft Medjool dates, pitted and diced*

Crushed toasted pistachios, for garnish

**If your dates are not soft, soak them in warm water for 5 to 10 minutes.*

Preheat the oven to 350°F and grease an 8×8-inch baking dish. Line the bottom and two of the sides with a sheet of parchment paper.

In a medium bowl, whisk together the all-purpose and whole wheat flours, baking powder, cinnamon, ginger, salt, baking soda, and cardamom.

In a large bowl, whisk together the brown sugar, eggs, applesauce, vegetable oil, and vanilla. Stir in the carrots.

Add the dry ingredients to the wet ingredients and mix until just combined. Fold in the dates.

Transfer the batter to the prepared pan and smooth the top. Bake for 32 to 37 minutes, or until a toothpick inserted comes out clean. Let cool in the pan for 15 minutes before turning out and transferring to a wire rack to cool completely.

RECIPE AND INGREDIENTS CONTINUE

Tangy Tahini Frosting

3 ounces full-fat, brick-style cream cheese, softened

1½ tablespoons tahini

1¾ cups powdered sugar, sifted if lumpy

1 tablespoon fresh lemon juice

¼ teaspoon vanilla extract

Pinch of sea salt

Make the tangy tahini frosting: In a large bowl, beat the cream cheese and tahini with an electric mixer until smooth. Add the powdered sugar, lemon juice, vanilla, and salt and mix until smooth, stopping and scraping down the sides of the bowl with a spatula as needed. (If you don't have an electric mixer, you can make this frosting by hand with a spatula—it will just take some elbow grease!)

Spread the frosting in a thick layer on top of the cooled cake. Garnish with crushed pistachios, slice, and serve.

SERVES **9**

VEGAN: Mix 3 tablespoons ground flaxseed with ½ cup water. Let thicken for 5 minutes, then add to the recipe in place of the eggs. Increase the baking powder to 1 tablespoon. Increase the bake time to 35 to 40 minutes. Use brick-style vegan cream cheese in the frosting (we like Violife). Spreadable vegan cream cheese from a tub will give the frosting a runnier, glaze-like texture.

ZESTY RICOTTA MUFFINS

WITH LEMON GLAZE

I grew up in a muffin family. Most days of the week, we had muffins on hand, and most mornings before school, I ate two for breakfast. There's something deeply comforting to me about having a muffin nearby. Growing up, I mostly had chocolate chip, but as I got older, I became less of a chocolate person (I know—gasp) and more of a lemon person (big surprise). Nowadays, these tender lemon muffins are exactly what I crave as a breakfast treat or an afternoon snack. *Bonus: They freeze well!*

2 cups all-purpose flour, spooned and leveled (see page 267)

2 teaspoons baking powder

½ teaspoon baking soda

½ teaspoon sea salt

1 cup whole milk ricotta cheese

2 large eggs

¾ cup maple syrup

½ cup extra-virgin olive oil, plus more for the pan

¼ cup fresh lemon juice

2 tablespoons lemon zest, plus more for garnish

1 teaspoon vanilla extract

Lemon Glaze

1 cup powdered sugar, sifted if lumpy

1 tablespoon fresh lemon juice, plus more as needed

Preheat the oven to 400°F and grease a 12-cup muffin tin or line it with muffin liners.

In a medium bowl, whisk together the flour, baking powder, baking soda, and salt.

In a large bowl, whisk together the ricotta, eggs, maple syrup, olive oil, lemon juice and zest, and vanilla.

Add the dry ingredients to the wet ingredients and mix until just combined. Use a ⅓-cup measuring cup to evenly divide the batter among the muffin cups.

Bake for 15 to 18 minutes, or until a toothpick inserted into the center of the muffins comes out clean. Let cool in the pan for 10 minutes, then transfer to a wire rack to cool completely.

Make the lemon glaze: In a small bowl, whisk together the powdered sugar and lemon juice to create a thick, smooth glaze. If needed, add more lemon juice, 1 teaspoon at a time, to help the glaze come together.

Drizzle over the cooled muffins and garnish with lemon zest. Enjoy right away or store in an airtight container at room temperature for up to 3 days. These muffins also freeze well for up to 3 months.

MAKES **12** *MUFFINS*

ICE CREAM *Sundaes*

What better way to close out this book than with a fun ice cream sundae bar? It has all kinds of toppings—saucy, spicy, crunchy, herby, and tangy—to make your sundae pop. Make one, make a few, or make them all—mix, match, and discover your favorite combinations.

Hint: Just don't skip the miso peanut caramel sauce.

SAUCY COMPONENTS

CHOCOLATE TAHINI SAUCE

½ cup dark chocolate chips

½ cup extra-virgin olive oil

6 tablespoons tahini

¼ cup maple syrup

⅛ teaspoon sea salt

In a small saucepan, combine the chocolate chips, olive oil, tahini, maple syrup, and salt. Cook, stirring, over low heat for 1 minute, or until the chocolate chips are melted and the mixture comes together into a smooth sauce.

YIELD: ABOUT 1 CUP

MISO PEANUT CARAMEL SAUCE

½ cup creamy natural peanut butter

3 tablespoons maple syrup

1 tablespoon white miso paste

1 teaspoon vanilla extract

½ cup plus 2 tablespoons unsweetened almond milk, plus more as needed

In a small saucepan, combine the peanut butter, maple syrup, miso, and vanilla. Cook, stirring, over low heat until the miso is incorporated. Gradually add the almond milk while whisking and continue to whisk for 1 minute, or until the sauce is smooth. Add more almond milk, 1 tablespoon at a time, as needed to reach a drizzleable consistency.

YIELD: ABOUT ¾ CUP

SPICY COMPONENTS

PINK PEPPERCORN CHOCOLATE-COVERED PRETZELS

½ cup dark chocolate chips

1 teaspoon coconut oil

¾ cup salted pretzel twists

1 to 2 tablespoons pink peppercorns, roughly crushed

Line a baking sheet with parchment paper.

In a small bowl, combine the chocolate chips and coconut oil. Microwave for 1 to 3 minutes, stirring every 20 seconds, or until smooth.

Dip the pretzels into the melted chocolate one at a time, then transfer to the baking sheet and sprinkle with the peppercorns. Set aside for 1 to 1½ hours, or until the chocolate is firm.

YIELD: ABOUT 1 CUP

SPICY PECANS

2 tablespoons brown sugar

1½ teaspoons water

¼ teaspoon cayenne pepper

⅛ teaspoon cinnamon

⅛ teaspoon sea salt

¾ cup raw pecans

Line a baking sheet with parchment paper.

In a small skillet, stir together the brown sugar, water, cayenne, cinnamon, and salt. Cook over medium heat for 1 minute, or until the sugar dissolves and the mixture bubbles. Add the pecans and cook, stirring, for another 1 to 2 minutes, or until well coated.

Spread the pecans evenly on the baking sheet and set aside for 1 hour, or until cool and crisp.

YIELD: ¾ CUP

CRUNCHY COMPONENTS

MAPLE SEA SALT POPCORN

1 tablespoon vegetable oil or other neutral oil

⅓ cup popcorn kernels

1 tablespoon unsalted butter, melted

2 tablespoons maple syrup

1 teaspoon flaky sea salt

Line a baking sheet with parchment paper.

Heat the vegetable oil in a large lidded pan over medium-high heat. Add the popcorn and cook until it starts to pop. Cover and reduce the heat. Cook, shaking the pan occasionally, for 2 to 3 minutes, or until the popping stops.

Remove from the heat and add the butter, maple syrup, and flaky sea salt. Toss to coat and spread evenly on the baking sheet. Set aside for 15 to 30 minutes, or until dry.

YIELD: ABOUT 6 CUPS

HONEY PEANUT CLUSTERS

½ cup unsalted peanuts

1 tablespoon honey

½ teaspoon melted coconut oil

¼ teaspoon vanilla extract

⅛ teaspoon sea salt

Preheat the oven to 350°F and line a baking sheet with parchment paper.

Place the peanuts on the baking sheet. Drizzle with the honey, coconut oil, and vanilla and sprinkle with the salt. Toss to coat and clump together in a single layer in the center of the baking sheet.

Bake for 10 minutes, or until the honey is bubbling and lightly browned. Set aside for 30 minutes, or until crisp, then break into clusters.

YIELD: ABOUT ⅔ CUP

TANGY COMPONENTS

STRAWBERRY BALSAMIC SAUCE

1 pound strawberries, hulled and chopped

2 tablespoons cane sugar

1 teaspoon balsamic vinegar

Pinch of sea salt

In a medium saucepan, combine the strawberries, sugar, balsamic vinegar, and salt. Cook, stirring, over medium heat until the sugar dissolves, then cook, stirring occasionally, for 10 minutes, or until the strawberries are soft and surrounded by thick juices.

YIELD: ABOUT 1½ CUPS

CHERRY POMEGRANATE SAUCE

2 pounds pitted cherries, thawed if frozen

¼ cup cane sugar

2 tablespoons pomegranate molasses

Pinch of sea salt

Measure 1 cup of the cherries and set aside.

In a large skillet, combine the remaining cherries, the sugar, pomegranate molasses, and salt. Cook, stirring, over medium heat for 1 minute, or until the sugar dissolves, then simmer, stirring occasionally, for 20 minutes. Add the reserved 1 cup cherries and continue to cook, stirring occasionally, for another 10 minutes to reduce the cherry juices slightly.

Set aside to cool to room temperature, then transfer to an airtight container and chill in the refrigerator until ready to serve.

YIELD: ABOUT 2 CUPS

HERBY COMPONENTS

MINTY SIMPLE SYRUP

½ cup water

½ cup cane sugar

1 cup fresh mint leaves

Heat the water and sugar in a small saucepan over medium heat. Cook, stirring occasionally, for 2 minutes, or until the sugar dissolves. Remove from the heat and add the mint leaves. Cover and steep for 20 minutes, then strain to remove the mint. Chill in the refrigerator until ready to serve.

YIELD: ½ CUP

LEMON PISTACHIO COOKIE CRUMBLES

Lemon Pistachio Cookies with Basil (page 307)

Crumble and use as a sundae topping!

EXTRAS

WHITE BASMATI OR JASMINE RICE

1 cup dry white basmati or jasmine rice, rinsed

1½ cups water

1 teaspoon extra-virgin olive oil

In a medium saucepan, combine the rice, water, and olive oil. Bring to a boil, then cover, reduce the heat, and simmer for 15 minutes, or until the water is absorbed. Remove from the heat and let sit, covered, for 10 minutes. Fluff with a fork.

YIELD: 3 CUPS COOKED

SHORT-GRAIN BROWN RICE

1 cup dry short-grain brown rice, rinsed

2 cups water

1 teaspoon extra-virgin olive oil

In a medium saucepan, combine the brown rice, water, and olive oil. Bring to a boil, then cover, reduce the heat, and simmer for 45 minutes, or until the water is absorbed. Remove from the heat and let sit, covered, for 10 minutes. Fluff with a fork.

YIELD: 3 CUPS COOKED

FARRO OR WHEAT BERRIES

1 cup dry farro or wheat berries, rinsed

Bring a medium pot of water to a boil. Add the grains, reduce the heat, and simmer, uncovered, until tender, 9 to 11 minutes for quick-cooking farro; 25 to 40 minutes for whole farro or soft wheat berries; and 45 to 60 minutes for hard wheat berries. Add more water to the pot as needed if the grains start to dry out. Drain.

YIELD: 3 CUPS COOKED

COOKED CHICKPEAS OR BEANS

1 cup dry chickpeas or beans

Place the chickpeas or beans in a large bowl. Discard any stones or debris. Cover with 2 to 3 inches of water and soak at room temperature for 8 hours or overnight. Drain and rinse. Place the soaked beans in a large pot and cover with 2 inches of water. Bring to a boil. Reduce the heat and simmer, uncovered, stirring occasionally, for 45 minutes to 2 hours, or until tender. Add more water to the pot as needed if the beans start to dry out. The timing will depend on the type and freshness of your beans.

YIELD: 3 CUPS COOKED

COOKED LENTILS

1 cup dry green or French green lentils, rinsed

Place the lentils in a medium pot of water. Bring to a boil. Reduce the heat and simmer, uncovered, stirring occasionally, for 17 to 20 minutes, or until tender but not mushy. Drain.

YIELD: 2½ TO 3 CUPS COOKED

BAKED TOFU

14 ounces high-protein tofu, patted dry and cubed or cut into planks

2 tablespoons tamari

1½ teaspoons avocado oil

½ teaspoon sriracha

1 tablespoon cornstarch

Preheat the oven to 425°F and line a baking sheet with parchment paper.

Place the tofu on the baking sheet. Drizzle with the tamari, avocado oil, and sriracha and sprinkle with the cornstarch. Toss to coat and spread evenly on the baking sheet. Bake for 20 to 25 minutes, or until browned around the edges.

SOFT-BOILED EGGS

4 large eggs

Bring a medium pot of water to a gentle simmer. Using a slotted spoon, carefully lower the eggs into the water and simmer for 7 minutes. Drain and rinse under cold water.

Tap the bottom of each egg to crack the shell. Carefully slide a small spoon in and around each egg to loosen and remove it from the shell.

CREMA

⅔ cup whole milk Greek yogurt

3 tablespoons mayonnaise

1 tablespoon fresh lemon or lime juice

Heaping ¼ teaspoon onion powder

¼ teaspoon garlic powder

⅛ teaspoon sea salt

In a medium bowl, stir together the yogurt, mayonnaise, lemon juice, onion powder, garlic powder, and salt. Season to taste and chill in the refrigerator until ready to serve.

YIELD: ABOUT 1 CUP

VEGAN: Replace the Greek yogurt with ¾ cup blended silken tofu. Use vegan mayo. Omit the salt and season to taste.

HOMEMADE HUMMUS

1½ cups cooked chickpeas, drained and rinsed (page 320)

⅓ cup smooth tahini

⅓ cup water, plus more as needed

2 tablespoons extra-virgin olive oil

2 tablespoons fresh lemon juice

1 garlic clove

½ teaspoon sea salt

In a high-speed blender, place the chickpeas, tahini, water, olive oil, lemon juice, garlic, and salt. Blend until very smooth, using the blender baton and adding more water as needed to reach your desired consistency.

YIELD: ABOUT 1 CUP

WHIPPED TOFU

14 ounces extra-firm tofu, drained

3 tablespoons fresh lemon juice

2 tablespoons extra-virgin olive oil

½ garlic clove

½ teaspoon sea salt

In a food processor, place the tofu, lemon juice, olive oil, garlic, and salt and pulse until creamy.

YIELD: ABOUT 2 CUPS

BASIL WHIPPED TOFU

1 cup Whipped Tofu (see above)

1½ teaspoons fresh lemon juice

¼ teaspoon sea salt

1½ cups fresh basil leaves

In a food processor, place the whipped tofu, lemon juice, and salt. Pulse until combined, then add the basil and pulse until the whipped tofu has green flecks.

YIELD: ABOUT 1 CUP

VEGAN LEMON CAPER MAYO

½ cup vegan mayonnaise

¼ cup silken tofu

1 tablespoon chopped fresh chives

2 teaspoons capers

1 teaspoon fresh lemon juice

½ teaspoon Dijon mustard

½ garlic clove

In a food processor, place the vegan mayonnaise, tofu, chives, capers, lemon juice, mustard, and garlic. Pulse until smooth and creamy.

YIELD: ABOUT ¾ CUP

HOMEMADE PIZZA DOUGH

¾ cup warm water, plus more as needed

1½ teaspoons maple syrup

1 (¼-ounce) package active dry yeast (2¼ teaspoons)

2 cups all-purpose flour, spooned and leveled (see page 267), plus more as needed

1 teaspoon sea salt

1 tablespoon plus 1 teaspoon extra-virgin olive oil

In a small bowl, stir together the water, maple syrup, and yeast. Set aside for 5 minutes, or until the yeast is foamy.

In the bowl of a stand mixer fitted with the dough hook, place the flour and salt. Mix on medium speed until combined. Add the yeast mixture and 1 tablespoon of the olive oil. Mix on medium speed for 5 to 6 minutes, or until the dough forms a ball around the hook. If the dough is too dry to form a ball, add water, 1½ teaspoons at a time, until the mixture comes together. If the dough is too sticky, add a little more flour.

Turn the dough out onto a lightly floured surface and gently knead into a smooth ball.

Brush a large bowl with the remaining 1 teaspoon olive oil and place the dough inside. Cover with plastic wrap and set aside to rise for about 1 hour, or until the dough has doubled in size.

Turn the dough out onto a lightly floured surface. Stretch into a large circle or oval, then top and bake according to the pizza recipe you are using, typically 11 to 15 minutes in a 500°F oven, or until the crust is browned.

YIELD: ABOUT 1 POUND

THANK YOU

To the *Love & Lemons* readers, thank you for cooking along with me for so many years. I am deeply grateful to be able to create recipes for you.

To my co-author, Phoebe Moore—I believe this is our best collection of recipes yet. I had so much fun creating this book with you, and I am thankful for your dedication to all things *Love & Lemons*.

To Trina Bentley, my friend, thank you for helping create another gorgeous book. And to you and Stephanie Worthington, thank you for the beautiful illustrations—you truly outdid yourselves.

To my wonderful photo team, you are simply the best. Eva Kolenko, Marian Cooper Cairns, Genesis Vallejo, Natalie Drobny, and Paige Arnett—thank you all. I am so grateful for our talented girl gang team.

To Judy Linden, thank you for being my number one supporter and for guiding me through each book.

To Lucia, thank you for your enthusiasm and encouragement around my book ideas. And thank you to the hardworking Avery and Penguin Canada teams for your kind support, especially Andrea Magyar, Farin Schlussel, Carla Iannone, Casey Maloney, Alyssa Adler, Isabel McCarthy, and Ashley Tucker.

Thank you to Jack Mathews and Alex Rocklin for your thoughtful feedback—and for making sure leftovers never went to waste.

To the rest of my family—Ollie, Mom, Dad, Karen, Josh, Liam, and Tessa—thank you for taste-testing so many recipes. And to my uncle Phil and aunt Judy, who have cheered along this L&L journey from the beginning.

Finally, thank you to Sophia Simota for your social media and video expertise, to Joanna Keohane for testing another book with me, and to Jessica Mathews for keeping my kitchen organized.

Note: Page numbers in **bold** indicate highlighted components. Page numbers (in parentheses) indicate recipes and tips featuring highlighted components. Page numbers in *italics* indicate photos of recipes.

A

B

D

E

I

J

K

L

M

Q

R

S

T